VOLUME 4

Miss Brenda's

BEDTIME STORIES

This book is lovingly
presented to

_____

By: _____

On this special occasion

_____

Date: _____

Miss Brenda's
BEDTIME
STORIES

BRENDA WALSH

Based on
True Character-Building Stories
for the Whole Family!

3ABN BOOKS

Three Angels Broadcasting Network
P.O. Box 220, West Frankfort, Illinois
www.3ABN.org

Pacific Press® Publishing Association
Nampa, Idaho
Oshawa, Ontario, Canada
www.pacificpress.com

Design/Layout: Chrystique Neibauer "CQ" I cqgraphicdesign.com
Cover Photography: David B. Sherwin
Project Coordinator: Mellisa Hoffman I finaleditservices.com
All images used under license from Shutterstock.com, unless otherwise noted.
Other inside photos, unless otherwise noted, have been provided by the author.

The author assumes full responsibility for the accuracy of all facts and quotations as cited in this book.

Additional copies of this book are available from two locations:

Adventist Book Centers®: Call toll-free 1-800-765-6955 or visit http://www.adventistbookcenter.com.

3ABN: Call (618) 627-4651 or visit http://www.store.3abn.org.

3ABN Books is dedicated to bringing you the best in published materials consistent with the mission of Three Angels Broadcasting Network. Our goal is to uplift Jesus Christ through books, audio, and video materials by our family of 3ABN presenters. Our in-depth Bible study guides, devotionals, biographies, and lifestyle materials promote whole person health and the mending of broken people. For more information, call 618-627-4651 or visit 3ABN's Web site: www.3ABN.org.

Scripture quotations marked NIV are from the HOLY BIBLE, NEW INTERNATIONAL VERSION®. Copyright © 1973, 1978, 1984 by International Bible Society. Used by permission of Zondervan Publishing House. All rights reserved.

Scriptures quoted from NKJV are from The New King James Version, copyright © 1979, 1980, 1982, Thomas Nelson, Inc., Publishers.

Scripture quotations marked NLT are taken from the Holy Bible, New Living Translation, copyright © 1996, 2004, 2007. Used by permission of Tyndale House Publishers, Inc., Wheaton, Illinois 60189. All rights reserved.

Scripture quotations marked KJV are from the King James Version of the Bible.

Library of Congress Cataloging-in-Publication Data:

Walsh, Brenda, 1953-
Miss Brenda's bedtime stories : true character building stories for the whole family! / Brenda Walsh.
     p. cm.
ISBN 13: 978-0-8163-2514-6 (hard cover)
ISBN 10: 0-8163-2514-6 (hard cover)
1. Christian children—Religious life—Anecdotes. 2. Families—Religious life—Anecdotes. I. Title. II. Title: Bedtime stories.
BV4571.3.W35 2011
249—dc22

                                                                    2011007590

11 12 13 14 15 • 5 4 3 2 1

DEDICATION

It is with heartfelt love that I dedicate volume four of Miss Brenda's Bedtime Stories *first to my dearest friend, Jesus, my Lord and Savior and then to my precious husband, Tim, and daughters, Rebecca and Linda Kay. It is my deepest desire that someday we'll all be gathered together in heaven as a family . . . without one missing!*

Tim Walsh

I couldn't imagine my life without my wonderful husband, Tim, who has faithfully stood by me in ministry throughout the years. His loving encouragement and support have been an enormous blessing! I will forever thank God for giving me such a precious friend and lifelong companion to walk beside me on this journey through life. *"Tim, thank you for always being there for me, for tenderly supporting me, and for being my best friend here on earth! Honey, I love you with all my heart!"*

Rebecca Lynn

When Rebecca was born, I began to understand a little more about God's amazing love. It seems like only yesterday, she was a baby in my arms. Now she has grown into a beautiful, caring, and talented young woman. Truly, my heart overflows with love. She is an amazing mother to my two special grandsons, Michael and Jason. *"Becky, I feel so blessed to be your mom and I love you so very much! I can't imagine my life without you!"*

Linda Kay

Linda Kay is truly a "gift from God!" Doctors told me I couldn't have any more children, but God had other plans! She has given me more joy than I could have thought possible! She has an incredible sense of humor and charm that everyone is naturally drawn to and is beautiful inside and out! *"Linda Kay, you have filled my heart with so much happiness. No matter how old you are, you will always be my baby girl! I love you more than you could possibly know!"*

ACKNOWLEDGMENTS

With Special Thanks

Dr. Kay Kuzma

I want to thank Dr. Kay Kuzma for all her hours and hours spent editing *Miss Brenda's Bedtime Stories*. She is one of the most generous, kind, and talented people I know and these stories would not have been the same without her! I admire and respect her professionalism, creative writing skills, and her loving service for others. Her love for our Lord and Savior shines through in all she does. She has blessed my life in so many ways and I thank God for the gift of her friendship.

Brenda Walsh

Author Appreciation

I want to personally thank each of these best-selling authors for their generous contribution of stories. It is truly an honor and privilege to include them in this book. Each author was personally selected to be a part of *Miss Brenda's Bedtime Stories* because of their creative and professional writing style, incredible talent, and love for Jesus! To each of them, I extend my sincere and heartfelt thanks!

Jean Boonstra

John Bradshaw

Karen Collum

Kenneth Cox

Karen Holford

Kay Kuzma

Charles Mills

Seth Pierce

Pam Rhodes

Kay D. Rizzo

Nancy Rockey

Kimberley Tagert-Paul

Jerry D. Thomas

Nancy Van Pelt

Perri Wiggins

ACKNOWLEDGMENTS

With Heartfelt Thanks To . . .

MY STORY AND PHOTO TEAM: *Battle Creek Academy* for opening your doors for the cover photo shoot. *Mellisa Hoffman* for your project coordination, organizational skills, being the "spelling champ," tenacity to *getting the job done*, and your loyalty and friendship! *Hannah and Lance Hoffman* for your patience during all the long hours your mom spent working on the book project. *Dr. Buddy and Tina Houghtaling* for organizing and planning the cover photo shoot, and all the years you dedicated your life to *Kids' Time*! *Chrystique Neibauer* for the incredible layout and graphic design of the entire project, for extra long hours, patience, and being a friend I can count on! *Dave Sherwin* for volunteering your time to photograph each cover.

MY MINISTRY SUPPORT TEAM: *Carole Derry-Bretsch* for your love, support, constant Christian witness, and, most of all, for being my lifelong friend! *Peg O'Brien Bernhardt* for always being there for me, listening, believing in me, and for your love and friendship! *Marie Macri* for being a precious friend—always there for me. I love you dearly! *Rita Showers* for a lifetime of memories, friendship, and the best neighbor a girl could have! *Nancy Sterling* for being my mentor, looking out for my best interests, and for your loving friendship!

MY FAMILY: My precious husband, *Tim Walsh,* for never complaining about the time I spent working on this project, for your constant support, help, and patience, but most of all, for your unconditional love you give me every day! *Rebecca Lynn and Linda Kay* for your love and support and allowing me to share your stories. My parents, *James and Bernice Micheff,* for your prayers, letting my team take over your house, for endless hours finding photos, and for all those great meals! To my *sisters, brothers, grandsons, aunts, uncles, nieces, and nephews* for your patience and loving understanding concerning the many hours I spent working on this project, even though you would have preferred I was spending time with you! I am so very grateful for my precious family and love you with all my heart!

Those who shared their stories with me:

Dianne Affolter
Mary Le Grice
Marcia Lincoln
Shane Linder

Joanie Pierce
Ron Reese
Laura & Hannah Richardson
Kitty Thomas

3ABN Kids' Time

Miss Brenda & Maxwell

Brenda Walsh is a vivacious, loving, and generous Christian with a heart for ministry and a burning desire to share the love and joy of Jesus. When she started praying, "Lord, use me in a special way," God did! And the resulting, amazing miracle stories have been an inspiration to thousands across the world who have heard her dynamic presentations or read her attention-grabbing books. Her message is one of encouragement and hope to those who want to be used by God. Hearing Brenda is truly a life-changing experience whether it's at a women's ministries retreat, a prayer conference, a church-based weekend event, or a children's ministries seminar.

Brenda is best known as "Miss Brenda," the producer and host of **Kids' Time**, a popular daily children's program on Three Angels Broadcasting Network (3ABN). She is also a frequent guest on the 3ABN *Today* program, cooking and singing with her sisters, Linda and Cinda. Together they have authored vegan vegetarian cookbooks and recorded several gospel CDs. Brenda also has her own solo CD, **My Wonderful Lord**.

Brenda is the author of **Battered to Blessed**, her life story of being a victim of domestic violence, and **Passionate Prayer**, which features her own personal stories of answered prayer. She has also co-authored several books with her friend, Kay Kuzma.

Miss Brenda and Strings of Joy on the Kids' Time set

In addition to ministering to others, Brenda is a registered nurse, interior decorator, and floral designer. Brenda is married to Tim Walsh, has two grown daughters, Becky and Linda Kay, and two grandsons, Michael James and Jason Patrick.

www.kidstime4jesus.org

LESSON INDEX

TABLE OF CONTENTS

Stories can have power to touch us and change us. They can help us understand what another person is feeling and help us see things from a new perspective. They can help us understand "Why?" and see the reasoning behind "Be careful!" They can help us learn lessons without having to suffer from making mistakes! That's why Jesus taught by telling stories. He knew that stories help us understand.

This book is full of stories told for the same reasons. So much effort, love, and prayer have gone into collecting and preparing *Miss Brenda's Bedtime Stories*! Based on true stories contributed from people around the world, each one has been written especially for Miss Brenda by beloved and best-selling authors (and some written by Miss Brenda herself!). They are sure to be loved by children and treasured by parents and grandparents and all who read them.

Brenda has shared these stories to help kids everywhere develop strong characters, understand important lessons, and most important, learn to be a good friend of Jesus. These pages are full of stories that are heart-touching, soul-searching, fun-filled, adventurous, and meant to be shared!

May these stories bring laughter to the eyes, wisdom to the mind, and understanding to the heart of everyone who hears them. And may there be a double blessing of peace and joy to each grown-up who takes a few precious moments to share them with a child.

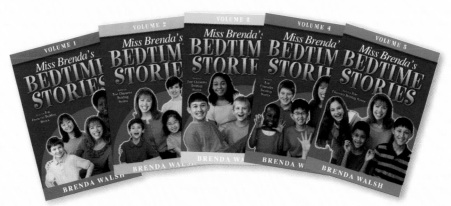

Be sure to collect all five volumes of
Miss Brenda's Bedtime Stories!

The Rocket Fire

Brendon and his younger brother, Byron, loved playing at Tommy's house. He lived right next to the "bush," which is what people who live in New South Wales, Australia, call a national park. The "bush" has lots of grass, shrubs, and giant eucalyptus trees. Because the eucalyptus sap is so sticky, they are also called gum trees. This was a favorite place for the three boys to race, ride bikes, and play soccer.

One day, after the boys tired of playing ball, Tommy sank to the ground, picked a blade of grass, and began chewing on it. "I'm bored," he sighed.

"Me too," Byron said, imitating Tommy.

Brendon's eyes brightened and his shoulders straightened. "I know what we can do. Let's make a rocket!"

Brendon loved rockets, especially rockets that produced loud noises. The bigger the *boom*, the better!

"How do we build a rocket?" Tommy's eyes flashed with interest.

"We can make a rocket out of wood and gum tree sap." Brendon always had such great ideas. "Does your dad have any scraps of wood in the garage?"

Tommy leaped to his feet. "Yeah, I think so. He was working on a cabinet last week. Let's go look!"

The boys raced to the garage and scattered in all directions. The hunt was on for anything that could be used to make a homemade rocket.

"Hey! Look what I found!" exclaimed Tommy. "An empty wooden crate. This will make a great launchpad."

Brendon and Tommy started filling the empty box with wood scraps, shavings, and anything else they thought they might need. Then they dragged it back to the clearing.

As Tommy began setting up the launchpad, Brendon collected the sticky sap from the gum trees to glue the wood pieces together.

"Look what I found in the garage," Byron said as he came up to where the boys were working and handed his brother a matchbox.

Tommy's eyes opened wide when Brendon opened the box. "Wow! There are still matches in there!"

The two older boys looked at the matches and then at one another. Tommy grinned at the younger boy. "Good job, Byron."

Byron smiled proudly at the compliment. Usually the older boys treated him more like a nuisance than a helper.

"This is super!" Brendon exclaimed with excitement. "With these matches we can get our rocket off the ground with a blast. Now, all we need is thrust . . . Wait! I've got a thruster!"

He reached into the left pocket of his jeans. "Gentlemen, I hold in my hand something we can use as rocket fuel." Slowly, he pulled his fist out of his pocket and waved it in the air to be certain he had both boys' attention. "A thruster," he announced, opening his hand dramatically to reveal a small cylinder no larger than a flashlight battery.

"How can that be a thruster?" Tommy's eyes narrowed.

"When I was younger," Brendon explained, "my dad and I were burning garbage in a steel barrel in the alleyway behind our house when we heard a loud explosion coming from inside the barrel. Dad said that there must have been a pressurized can in one of the trash bags. He said a pressurized can will explode in a fire regardless of what might have been inside it."

Continuing in his role as *Chief Rocket Scientist,* Brendon held up the cylinder for the boys to examine. "Of course, it would be very dangerous if this were a large can of something like hairspray, but this little can will be just big enough to be a perfect thruster."

Brendon could see Tommy and Byron were impressed with his scientific knowledge. "Yup. This little thruster will give us just the liftoff we need."

"So what is it?" asked Tommy.

Brendon eyed the cylinder with a look of superiority. "Oh, this is the aerosol container for Byron's medicine. My mom trusts me to make sure Byron takes his asthma medicine whenever he starts wheezing. Mom gave me a new one to use because this one was almost empty." Brendon removed Byron's fresh inhaler from his right pocket to show them. Then he held up the old container. "Lucky for us, this one is now empty."

Tommy and Byron *ooh*ed and *aah*ed as if it were made of solid gold.

Brendon pocketed the filled container and announced excitedly, "Come on guys! Let's build a rocket ship!"

The boys huddled over Brendon as he glued the wood slats together into the shape of a rocket. At last, the rocket was ready. Now, it was time for the launch. Brendon made a few final adjustments to the box they were using for the launchpad. Next, he placed Byron's empty inhaler on it and surrounded the canister with small rocks, wood shavings, and pieces of bark. "This is so the trajectory will maximize," Brendon explained to his audience. Finally, he placed the makeshift rocket in position.

The boys tingled with excitement as Commander Brendon signaled Tommy to begin the countdown just like a real launch at Cape Canaveral. Cupping his hands around his mouth, Tommy cleared his throat and took a deep breath.

"TEN!" Tommy shouted.

"NINE! Clear the launchpad!" Tommy backed up several steps. Brendon and Byron hovered over the rocket.

"EIGHT . . . Byron! I *said*, 'Clear the launchpad!' " Byron finally backed up and stood next to Tommy.

"SE-VEN!" Tommy made two words out of the number for emphasis.

"SIX! Man all battle stations!" Tommy continued.

"FIVE! Fire the engines!" Brendon ceremoniously struck the first match. It flared and immediately went out.

Tommy repeated his command. "FIVE! Fire the engines!" Brendon struck the second match against the box. Instead of lighting, the match head broke off and fell to the ground.

"This is harder than I thought," muttered Brendon to himself. His parents had forbidden him to play with matches, so he had never lit one before, but he had seen his dad and mom do it. *How hard can it be?*

"FIVE! Fire the engines!" Tommy commanded once more.

Brendon struck a third match next to the rocket ship. It flared. Immediately, the wood shavings burst into flame. Brendon leaped away from the launchpad, expecting an explosion.

Determined that their rocket would have a proper send-off, Tommy quickly completed his countdown. "Four . . . Three . . . Two . . . One . . . Liftoff!"

Instead of the dramatic liftoff and flight as anticipated, the three boys watched as their homemade aircraft sat motionless on the smoldering launchpad. What a disappointment! Their shoulders drooped.

"Oh well, we tried," Brendon sighed. "I can't figure out what went wrong."

Brendon started toward the dud of a rocket. *BOOM!* The thruster exploded, sending dozens of burning wood shavings into the air. Landing in the surrounding bushes and on the dry leaf-covered ground, they ignited into small fires. Aghast, the boys watched as the burning blaze began to devour the sticks and dry leaves.

"Quick! Stomp them out!" Brendon sprang into action, stomping with both feet on one little fire and then jumping onto the next.

Tommy joined him and began hopping and jumping on the little bonfires. Within seconds, the tiny sparks became bigger fires. Frightened, Brendon and Tommy continued to dance on the spreading flames.

Suddenly, Byron started to scream so loudly that Tommy thought he might have caught himself on fire. He hadn't, but Byron continued shrieking in terror just the same.

"Byron!" Brendon shouted. "Do you want Tommy's mom to hear you?"

"Yes!" he said emphatically. Gasping for fresh air, he bellowed even louder, "Burning bush!"

Hearing the screams, Tommy's mother came running across the yard. When she saw the smoke, she yelled, "Dad! Get the extinguisher! Quick! The boys have started a fire!"

An hour later, three very somber boys and a very tired Dad and Mom sat on a log in the middle of a large patch of blackened bush and soggy smoldering leaves.

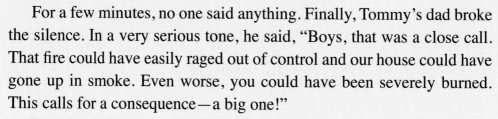

Brendon looked around and gazed at the burned ground, at Tommy's house, and at the acres of trees that could have been destroyed. He shuddered at what might have happened if Tommy's mother had not heard Byron scream. He felt responsible since it was his idea.

For a few minutes, no one said anything. Finally, Tommy's dad broke the silence. In a very serious tone, he said, "Boys, that was a close call. That fire could have easily raged out of control and our house could have gone up in smoke. Even worse, you could have been severely burned. This calls for a consequence—a big one!"

Brendon looked up at Tommy's dad. His voice quivered. "Mr. Martin, I lit the match and it was my thruster that caused the explosion. It was my fault and I'm the only one who should be punished."

"Wait a minute," said Tommy. "No one forced me. It was my fault too. But, Byron is too little to know any better."

Brendon stared at the ground while Tommy chewed his fingernails. Trembling, they waited to hear what their fate might be. They knew they deserved to have their privileges taken away—maybe even for a whole year. Or they might even get something worse.

"You're right," Dad agreed. "Byron is too young to be held responsible and I think the scare was punishment enough for him. But, Tommy, you and Brendon are old enough to know better. You deserve to be punished.

"Here's what I'm going to do. The New South Wales Rural Fire

Service has a training program for boys twelve to sixteen years of age. They teach about fire prevention, fire safety, and firefighting techniques.

"Brendon, I'm going to speak with your dad, and if he agrees, I'm going to enroll both you and Tommy. You will also have to help with the chores at the fire station, like cleaning the fire engines, sweeping, picking up trash, and, yes, even cleaning the toilets! I believe when you finish your training you will have learned the valuable lesson to never, ever, play with fire again!" ■

> *Likewise the tongue is a small part of the body, but it makes great boasts. Consider what a great forest is set on fire by a small spark.*
> —James 3:5, NIV

Piano Disaster

"Natalie," Mom called. "Time to practice the piano!"

Natalie had just unwrapped two of her favorite Christmas ornaments and was setting them on the table. "Mom," she complained, "I'm not done taking all the decorations out of the box yet. Please, could I just finish it first?"

"Natalie," Mom sighed, "you always have an excuse. I want you to start practicing right now!"

"Yes, Mom," Natalie answered. She slumped down on the piano bench and flipped through her music book. *Oh,* she thought, *I don't want to practice piano right now! It's almost Christmas and here I am, stuck on this bench!* Unhappily she banged on the keys of the piano, playing loud and fast. Soon, she started to like the sound of it. She played faster and louder, banging and rushing her way through the song.

Photo taken by Jean Boonstra

"Natalie!"

Natalie jumped a little at the sound

of Mom's voice. "Yes," she hollered, still banging loudly.

Mom appeared from around the corner and glanced over Natalie's shoulder, looking at her music. "That is not how that piece is supposed to sound! I don't think the composer himself would recognize what you're playing."

Natalie frowned and closed her book.

"I know that it's nearly Christmas," Mom said, "but you still need to focus. Your Level Three piano test is coming up in March."

"Oh, Mom, I have lots of time!" Natalie answered. "You can trust me to learn this. I promise I will."

"Can I?" Mom asked.

Natalie felt the frustration bubbling up inside. "Mom! I'm twelve years old. Why can't you trust me? Stop treating me like a baby." She squirmed on the piano bench.

"What makes you think I treat you like a baby?" Mom answered.

Natalie sat up straight and answered in her calmest voice, "You don't trust that I'll learn my piano pieces on my own. And . . . well . . . I have to go to bed at the same time as my little sister. It's embarrassing!"

"So," Mom answered, "do you want me to trust you more at practice time?"

Natalie nodded.

"OK. I'll trust you to practice properly. I'm still going to remind you if you forget though."

"Thanks, Mom," Natalie answered. She smiled and flipped back through her music book. Slowly and carefully, she tried the piece again. *I can do this,* she told herself. *I have to show Mom and Dad that I really can!*

Photo taken by: Jean Boonstra

Natalie practiced faithfully for the rest of the week. However, staying focused over Christmas break was more difficult than she had imagined. After that, there was her friend Haley's birthday party, Rachel's sleepover, and the field trip to the Discovery Science Center to plan for! The days quickly slipped by.

Then one morning as Natalie was getting ready for school, she began to panic. *Oh, no! Only one week until my piano test!* she thought as she jumped out of bed. After dashing down the stairs, she grabbed her stack of books off of the piano bench. She had a terrible sick feeling in her stomach as she flipped quickly through the pages. Taking a deep breath, Natalie closed her eyes. "Think, think, think!" she whispered to herself. Then she had an idea. Running to the family room, she turned on the computer.

Photo taken by: Jean Boonstra

"Natalie," Mom asked with a yawn, "what are you doing up so early?"

"Making myself a practice chart," she answered without looking up. Her fingers raced over the computer keys. "I need to make sure I'm ready for my music test!" When the printer spat out the chart she had made, Natalie grabbed it and took it to the piano. *Now, if I just follow this plan each day, I'll be OK.* She played each of her pieces over and over again and then put a little check mark on her chart when she finished practicing each one.

All too soon, the day of the test had arrived. Natalie anxiously clutched her books as she got out of the car and walked up to the testing center. When her name was called, she jumped nervously. Trying to encourage her, Dad squeezed her hand. "Sweetie, I love you. Don't worry." Natalie felt her legs wobble a little as she walked to the testing room.

"Hello, Natalie," said a woman with a kind smile. "I'm Mrs. Sanderson. I'll be listening to you play to see what you've learned this year. If you are ready, you'll be able to advance to the next level."

"OK," Natalie answered shyly, sitting down on the unfamiliar piano bench.

"Let's hear what you have for me today," said Mrs. Sanderson.

Natalie began to play; but after just a few notes, her brain froze. She couldn't remember what came next. *Oh no!* she thought. A panicky feeling washed over her.

"Try again," Mrs. Sanderson said as she took notes on the test evaluation sheet.

Natalie started playing and again she couldn't remember the rest of the piece. "May I start once more?" she asked sheepishly, her cheeks hot with embarrassment.

"Sure. Start from the top," Mrs. Sanderson answered.

Natalie breathed a little prayer and began again. This time, her fingers remembered what to do. She played a few wrong notes near the end, but she was relieved when she made it all the way through.

The whole test lasted less than fifteen minutes. When it was over, Mrs. Sanderson said, "Thank you, Natalie. You may go now."

Natalie nodded politely and slowly got up from the piano bench. She tried hard not to cry.

Once they were outside, though, the tears began to flow. "Oh, Dad, that was a DISASTER!"

"What happened, honey?" he asked tenderly

"I had to start one piece three times!" Natalie groaned.

Dad let out a low whistle. "Now, that isn't good, is it?"

"Dad," Natalie cried, "I just want to get out of here!"

Natalie barely said a word on the way home. When they arrived, she ran inside and went straight up to her room. All day long, she felt like a terrible failure. She couldn't even look at the piano. The memory of her piano test was too awful.

After dinner, she picked up a book and tried to read, hoping to forget about her terrible day.

"Natalie!" Mom called from her office. "Please come here. I want you to read this. It's an e-mail from your piano teacher."

Natalie read the e-mail and her heart seemed to leap for joy! "She says that all her students passed their piano tests today. That means that I passed!" Natalie wrapped her arms happily around her mom's neck. "I can't believe it!"

Natalie dashed over to the piano. Returning with her practice chart, she placed it on her mom's desk. "Mom," she said, "the only thing that helped me to pass the test was that I followed my chart and practiced a lot this week. Can you imagine how much better I would have done if I had practiced that carefully all year long? I would have received a certificate with honors. Well, this year I am going to practice like you've never heard me practice before! Next year, I *will* get honors! Just wait and see!"

THIS CERTIFIES THAT
Natalie Boonstra

HAS SUCCESSFULLY COMPLETED
PIANO LEVEL THREE

illustrated by: cxgraphicdesign.com

Mom leaned over and kissed her on the forehead. "Sweetie, I think that you've just earned yourself a later bedtime!"

Natalie grinned. "Well, maybe something good came out of my piano disaster after all!" ■

> *Let us not become weary in doing good,*
> *for at the proper time we will reap a harvest if*
> *we do not give up.*
> —Galatians 6:9, NIV

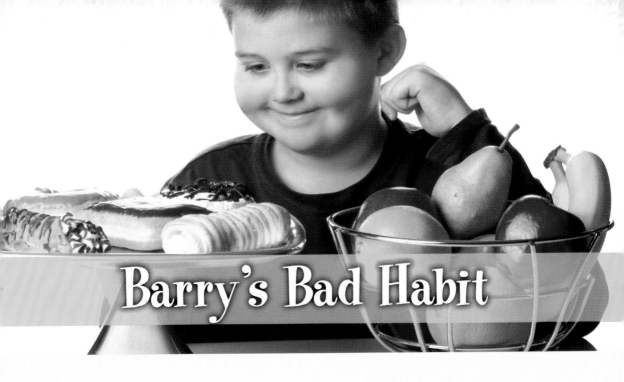

Barry's Bad Habit

Barry had a bad habit. He ate too much. When he saw food, he just had to taste it. And desserts nearly jumped off of the dish and into his mouth. He just couldn't seem to help himself, not even when his friends teased him about being fat.

"You shouldn't eat so much." "You need to lose weight." "Eat more fruits and vegetables." Barry had heard those words so often that he dreaded eating in front of anyone for fear he would get another lecture. Instead of helping him, hearing people criticize the way he ate just made him mad. Instead of eating less, he felt like eating more.

He knew people were just trying to help—after all, it was obvious he was a few pounds overweight—but he just couldn't say No to food.

"Hey, guess what, Barry? My birthday's coming up," his friend Stan announced. "I want you to come to my party." Barry was excited. That's all he could think about for weeks. Stan was nice to him and made him feel special. Not all the kids in his class did.

When Barry got to the party, it seemed like most of the kids were already there. He felt a little shy. It was a swimming party, so he had his swimming suit in one bag and the gift for Stan in the other.

"What are you doing, Barry, bringing enough food for two?" Curt teased when he saw him enter the room.

"I have a present in one bag—and my swimming suit in the other." Barry tried to ignore the sarcastic comment and went over to the table to put his gift down where the other gifts were stacked. That's when he saw the big dish of chocolate-covered raisins—his favorite candy. He knew when it came to chocolate that he had a major problem: once he starting eating it, he couldn't stop. Knowing he would probably get teased if he ate too much, he quickly stuffed a handful in his mouth and went to find Stan.

But the temptation to nibble was stronger than his need to avoid the teasing, and when the rest of the kids went outside to go swimming, he plopped himself down by the bowl of chocolate-covered raisins . . . and ate them all!

Suddenly, he came to his senses. *What have I done?* But the candy was already gone. He felt guilty, fat, miserable, and sick to his stomach. Instead of having a good time at the party and swimming with the rest of the kids, all he wanted to do was go home. He ran into the house, picked up the phone, and dialed. "Mom," he said, "I don't feel good. Can you come and pick me up?"

When his mom pulled up in front of Stan's house, he grabbed his dry swimming suit—still in the bag—and ran out to the car. Stan saw him leaving and called out, "Hey, Barry, where are you going?"

But it was too late; Barry was already buckling his seat belt. As soon as Mom drove off, he began sobbing. "Mom, something's wrong with me. I just can't say No to food. Kids tease me because I'm fat. I hate myself! And you won't believe what I just did. I ate the whole bowl of chocolate-covered raisins!"

Mom listened. "Barry, honestly, I don't think you can change by yourself."

"What do you mean, Mom? I don't like the way I am."

"You've been eating everything you see for so long that it's become a bad habit. You do it automatically, without thinking. If you want to change, you have to retrain your brain—and to do that you're going to need help, big time help."

"OK," said Barry, "where do I find someone to help me retrain my brain?"

"You're going to have to discover the answer yourself," Mom replied. "I'll give you a clue. As soon as we get home, I want you to open your Bible and read Philippians, chapter four, and write down ideas that come to your mind as you're reading. Be sure to include the text in case you forget and have to look it up again."

"What does the Bible have to do with retraining my brain?" Barry looked puzzled.

"A lot! You'll see!"

As soon as Barry got home, he went to his room and found his Bible. "Let's see . . . " He tried to remember where Philippians was in the New Testament. *Galatians, Ephesians, Philippians . . . here it is,* he said to himself. He started reading chapter four. After he read verses four through eight, Barry wrote down, "Think positively." Then he wrote down, "Don't worry, be thankful, and tell God what you need, Philippians 4:6."

He read on. "Aha!" he said when he got to verse thirteen and then called to his mom. "I found it! I found it! It says, 'I can do all things through Christ who strengthens me,'" he shouted.

Mom rushed to his bedroom door wiping her wet hands on a towel. "That's great! What do you think it means?"

"It means that with Jesus, I can do anything. I can even break my bad habit!"

"And retrain your brain," added Mom. "Now you need a plan so you will know exactly how you're going to let Jesus help you. I just made a pizza. Let's eat first and do some brainstorming."

"*Ummm,* pizza sounds really good. Maybe not as good as the food I missed at Stan's party," Barry winked at his mom, "but then again— maybe better!" He laughed and started to load his plate with three slices of pizza. Suddenly, he stopped. "Mom, quick! I need a plan or I'm going to stuff myself again!"

"OK, first call on the Master of the universe to give you His power!"

"You mean, Jesus?"

"Of course! He has power over everything—even your bad habit—if you'll let Him. That's step one."

"OK," Barry said as he shut his eyes and prayed. "Dear Jesus, please give me Your power. Help me to say No when I'm tempted to eat too much. Amen."

"Barry, do you know what just happened?" asked Mom. "Jesus just sent ten thousand angels to help you resist temptation. Now, the next step is to get rid of the enemy."

"What enemy?"

"Who do you think tempts you to do things you shouldn't?"

"Satan?"

"Right. Knowing how to get rid of Satan is step two. You can find it in Luke 4:8, where Jesus is being tempted. You'll need to say the same thing Jesus said."

Quickly, Barry opened his Bible and read, "Get behind Me, Satan."

"What do you think that means?" Mom asked.

"I've got to tell Satan to beat it. Get out of here. Leave me alone!"

"OK, you now have step one and step two. Are you ready for step three? It's the clincher."

"What is it?"

"Get out of there yourself. Avoid temptation. Don't open the refrigerator door. Don't stand next to the bowl of candy or the cookie jar. When you're finished eating, excuse yourself from the table and do something else. When you start to think about food, make yourself think about something else by reading a good book, talking to a friend, getting a drink of water, or reading your Bible."

"I don't know if I can do that," Barry admitted.

"Then you're back to step one."

"You mean, I need to claim the Bible promise that 'I can do all things through Christ'?"

"You've got it! Jesus can strengthen your willpower. And here's the good news . . . if you follow this three-step plan every time you're tempted to eat, then you will be retraining your brain. Instead of going back for seconds, your brain will automatically go to step one and you'll have Jesus' power to say NO!"

Suddenly, a big smile spread across Barry's face. "Mom, thanks for showing me that this is a battle I can win. I know Jesus *will* help me break my bad habit." ■

I can do all things through Christ
who strengthens me.
—Philippians 4:13, NKJV

Goats for God

"That's beautiful, Kierra," Dad said as he watched her apply charcoal to the picture in front of her. "By the way, I have a great project I'm going to tell you about at family worship tonight."

"Oh, Dad, can't you tell me now?" Kierra pleaded.

"No," Dad answered with a twinkle in his eye, "you're just going to have to wait until tonight," he said as he smiled and headed out the door.

Kierra wondered what her father was planning. He was always coming up with great ideas, fun trips, or exciting projects. She could hardly wait until after supper when the family got together to sing, pray, and read stories.

She went back to her drawing. Mrs. Huntley, her art teacher, had suggested she give charcoal a try. She loved art, but this was the first time she had worked with charcoal. She had seen a picture in a magazine of a man holding a baby and decided she would try something

Illustrated by: cqgraphicdesign.com

similar. First, she sketched the outline and then she began using different art pencils and charcoal sticks to give her picture a three-dimensional quality. She had been working on it for some time. Now she was almost finished.

"It looks good enough to frame," her mom commented as she stood behind Kierra, admiring her work. "What are you going to do with it when it's finished?"

"I'm not sure, but thanks for the nice compliment," Kierra replied. "It reminds me of the song, 'He's Got the Whole World in His Hands.' I could hang it in my room to help me remember that God has me in His hands too."

Finally, it was worship time. "OK, Dad, tell us your idea. Are we going someplace special?"

"Not unless you're going to pay the way," smiled Dad. "I was thinking that instead of doing something for ourselves, maybe we could do something for someone else. Let me show you what I found on the Internet."

Both Kierra and her brother, Kobe, were curious as they sat down with Mom and Dad to see the computer screen. "I found an international aid organization that helps poor families. If we'd like to give ten dollars, we can feed a starving child in Africa for a week. Or we can give a gift of twenty-five dollars. That's enough to help a child in Bangladesh get off the streets. It will provide a home, education, medical care, and one good meal a day."

"Hey," Kobe said, "here's one about chickens. For thirty-five dollars we can buy enough chickens for a single mother in Tanzania so her family can start an egg business and support themselves."

"Or this one," said Kierra. "For fifty dollars we can buy a goat that can have babies, which can be sold to support a family in Tunisia, and then the goat can give milk for the children so they can be healthy. That's what I want to do. That's a gift that just keeps on giving!"

"Where's Tunisia?" asked Kobe.

"Here, let me Google it," Kierra said as she began typing on Dad's computer keypad. "Africa!" she announced. "In fact, it's the most northern country in Africa."

"What do you think?" Dad asked the rest of the family. "Shall we buy mission goats?"

"I'm in," said Mom.

"Me too," agreed Kobe.

"Now all we have to do is figure out how we're each going to raise our share of the money," Dad said.

"I'll weed gardens," offered Kobe.

"I can shave five dollars a week off my food budget," Mom said.

"I'll save all my loose change," Dad added

"Well, I'll pray about it," Kierra said. "I'm sure God will help me come up with a good idea."

The next day, Mrs. Huntley told Kierra that there was going to be an art sale at the local golf course and encouraged her to enter her charcoal drawing. "You are so talented, I'm sure your picture will sell right away," her teacher said.

"Well," said Kierra, "that's the answer to my prayer. If it does, I'll help buy some mission goats!"

When she got home, she told her father about the art sale.

"Oh, honey, that would be great," Dad said. "But I hear there are quite a few adults who enter that show, so there will be some pretty stiff competition. Your picture might not sell for very much."

"Well, I'm going to do my best and let God do the rest," Kierra laughed at her rhyme. With extra determination, Kierra spent most of her free time working on her charcoal drawing.

On the day of the contest, the pictures were sold by silent auction. Under each work of art was a "bid" card where people would write down their identification number and how much money they would be willing to pay for the picture. If another person liked that piece of art better, they would put down a higher bid.

Kierra watched as several people looked at her picture. Eventually, a person actually placed a bid of thirty-five dollars. She was excited! Then someone else put sixty dollars below that. Kierra couldn't believe someone would actually pay sixty dollars for something she had drawn.

But then again, she realized that this was God's picture. Shortly after that, a lady offered $125. Then, near the end of the art show, a man came by who had looked at Kierra's picture several times. He called to his wife. After the two studied Kierra's artwork, they both nodded at each other, and he wrote down $250. A few minutes later, the art exhibit closed and Kierra watched in amazement as the man wrote her a check for her charcoal picture.

ITEM: #063	
He's Got the Whole World in His Hands	
Charcoal Drawing	
Bidder #	Bid Amount
436	$35.00
252	$60.00
138	125.00
356	$250.00

Illustrated by: cqgraphicdesign.com

"So, what are you going to do with the money?" the man asked.

"I'm going to buy goats!" Kierra announced proudly.

"Goats!" exclaimed the man. "Why goats?"

"Our family has a mission project to buy female goats for poor families in Tunisia. The baby goats can be sold and then the mother goat will provide milk to keep the children healthy. Each goat costs fifty dollars. We were going to buy one or two, but you've made it possible for us to get five!"

Once again, the man looked at his wife. She smiled and he wrote an additional check for one hundred dollars. "Here," he said to Kierra, "add this to your money. My wife and I would like to buy two more mission goats."

That night, Kierra and her family celebrated God's blessings. "Here I thought we could buy one or two goats, and now Kierra's painting has made it possible for us to buy seven goats instead!" Dad exclaimed. "What do you say, kids? I bet if we work really hard and ask God to continue blessing this project, maybe we could get a few more!"

"Sounds good to me," Kobe pitched in. "Pulling weeds isn't so bad."

"I think I'll start on another charcoal picture," said Kierra.

"Well," said Mom, "as the saying goes, 'You can't outgive the Lord.'"

Dad laughed. "And you can't have too many goats for God!" ∎

> *Whoever sows sparingly will also reap sparingly, and whoever sows generously will also reap generously.*
> —2 Corinthians 9:6, NIV

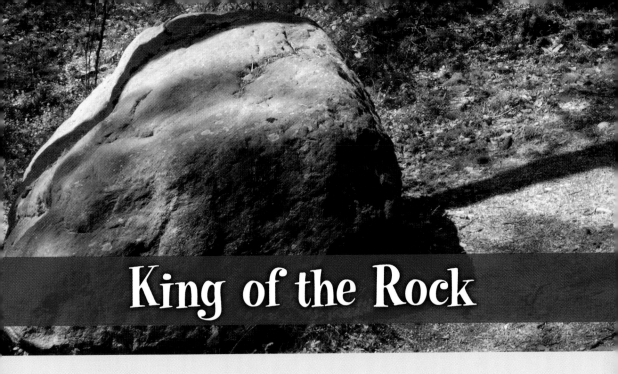

King of the Rock

Impatiently, Kyle listened to the sermon. "And God said, 'I will never leave you nor forsake you.'" Then to emphasize his point, Pastor Jim asked, "When is God going to leave you?"

The congregation answered in unison, "Never."

Kyle glanced up at the clock. *Church should be over soon.*

Once more the pastor asked, "Let me hear you say it again. When will God leave you?"

Kyle joined in with the rest and said with a loud voice, "NEVER!"

It was a good sermon, but Kyle's mind was on how much fun he was going to have hiking with the older boys that afternoon. Dad was the boys' club director, and even though Kyle was too young to join the club, Dad had promised that he could go.

At the church fellowship meal, Kyle stuffed a couple of oatmeal raisin cookies into his pocket to eat on the trail, then quickly changed into his hiking boots, and piled into the van with the other kids.

It took almost an hour to drive to the trailhead. Kyle resisted the temptation to ask, "Are we almost there?" He didn't want to act like an impatient little kid around the older guys. At the trailhead, Dad organized the boys into three groups, each with an adult counselor. Then he warned, "This state park is very big and has miles and miles of trails. It is extremely important that you stay close together so no one gets lost. If you should get separated, return to the spot where you last saw the group and stay put. Let us find you. Don't try to find us. Do you understand?"

Yeah, yeah, yeah, Kyle thought. *Come on. Let's get going!* The older boys were as eager to get started as he was. Finally, his father blew the whistle and shouted, "OK, boys. Let's move 'em out!"

Kyle hiked with his dad for a while, then he dropped behind to inspect a giant lichen-covered rock. He was soon distracted by a yellow and black butterfly flitting through the forest and decided to chase it. Coming back to the group, Kyle told Patrick, one of the older boys, about a snake hole he had stumbled across. "Probably was a chipmunk hole," Patrick insisted.

"No, I'm sure it was a snake hole. Maybe a rattler's!"

"You don't know that!" Patrick rolled his eyes.

"Yes, I do. Ya wanna see?"

"Naw." Patrick waved Kyle away and hurried to catch up with his friends.

I know it was a snake hole, Kyle sniffed, dropping to the back of the group. His eyes lit up when he spotted an enormous fallen tree off the side of the trail. Instantly, Kyle knew he had to climb on it. He scrambled onto the rough bark, stood up, and, balancing himself with his arms stretched out, he walked the full length of the log. At the far end, he spied a huge rock just made for climbing. He followed a narrow pathway around the rock until he came to a series of footholds to the top. He climbed up the side of the rock and shouted, "Look, guys! I'm king of the rock!"

But no one heard him. No one saw him because no one was in sight. Kyle looked back at the log he had been walking on. No one was there. Kyle looked north, he looked south, he looked east, he looked west. A tiny pinpoint of fear shot through him. Kyle shouted, "Hello! Anybody hear me?"

Kyle paused to listen, but the only sounds he could hear were of chirping birds and the wind blowing through the leaves of the trees. *Where did everyone go? Where is Dad?* He now had a big knot in the pit of his stomach as he half slid, half tumbled down the side of the rock.

He started to run and then stopped to get his bearings. "Where was that fallen tree?" he mumbled as he charged in the direction he thought was correct. As he stumbled through the underbrush, his father's warning played over and over again in Kyle's head, *"Stay with the group!"*

After what seemed like hours, Kyle stopped at a fork in the narrow pathway. He didn't remember any forks in the path that the group was on. He looked first one way and then the other. Nothing looked right. *Which path had they taken? Which way should I go?* Like it or not, Kyle was lost. A cold chill traveled up his spine. Never in his life had he felt so alone.

Kyle's imagination went wild. He began to think about giant black bears hiding behind tree trunks and rattlesnakes with foot-long fangs lurking in the bushes. When a small bird swooped out of a tree and cawed, Kyle jumped. He felt like crying.

That's when Kyle remembered Pastor Jim's sermon, "And God said, 'I will never leave you nor forsake you.' "

"I'm *not* alone," Kyle reminded himself. "God is always with me. He knows right where I am. And He knows where my dad is. It's no big deal to God." But just to be sure, Kyle closed his eyes in the middle of the narrow pathway and prayed, "Dear Jesus, I really messed up this time. I'm so scared. I don't know where I am, but You do. Please help me to find my dad and the other kids."

When he opened his eyes, Kyle examined both of the pathways that veered in opposite directions into the woods. *If the path on the left leads back to the fallen log,* he reasoned, *wouldn't that mean the path on the right will take me to where the group has gone?*

"Which one, dear Jesus?" Kyle whispered. "I can't just stand here alone in the woods!" That's when he remembered his dad's instruction, *"Stay put and we'll find you."* He hadn't obeyed his dad about staying with the group and look what had happened. But he could obey now and stay right where he was.

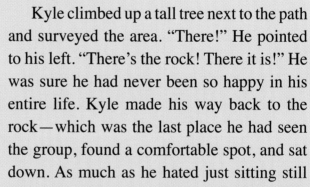

Kyle climbed up a tall tree next to the path and surveyed the area. "There!" He pointed to his left. "There's the rock! There it is!" He was sure he had never been so happy in his entire life. Kyle made his way back to the rock—which was the last place he had seen the group, found a comfortable spot, and sat down. As much as he hated just sitting still and waiting for his father, he knew that following his dad's advice was his wisest choice.

As he sat there, he thought about all the fun he was missing. If only he had obeyed his dad! He was getting hungry. He took out the cookies he had put in his pocket and started to nibble. He kicked at an anthill with his boot and watched the tiny creatures scurry to rebuild. Then he dropped some cookie crumbs and watched the

ants try to move them. When he grew bored with the ants, he studied a bee as it buzzed from one blossom of mountain laurel to the next. The warm sunlight on his back made him drowsy. He curled up on his side, put one hand beneath his head, and closed his eyes.

"Kyle! Kyle!"

Kyle jerked awake.

"Kyle! Where are you?"

"Dad?" Kyle jumped up. "Over here!"

As his father rounded a bend in the trail, Kyle ran into his open arms. His dad swept him off his feet and whirled around. "I'm so glad I found you. I was so worried!"

"Me too," Kyle admitted. "I'm sorry, Dad, for disobeying you and wandering away from the group."

His father gave him an extra hug. "I guess I should have kept a closer eye on you! I forgot you were younger than the rest."

"But I remembered what you said about staying put," Kyle stated.

"I'm sure glad you did," his father replied.

Side by side, Kyle and Dad hiked back to the vans where everyone was waiting. He couldn't wait to share his adventure with the others.

When Patrick asked if he had been scared in the woods all alone, Kyle replied, "You bet, especially at first. But then I remembered what Pastor Jim said in his sermon about how God promises never to leave us alone. Never!" he said with emphasis. "I just kept thinking about that promise, and I wasn't afraid anymore." ■

> *"I will never leave you nor forsake you."*
> — Hebrews 13:5, NKJV

Keeping Promises

"**M**om," Judy said as she ran into the kitchen. "Mrs. Costello asked me to take care of her pets next weekend while she visits her son. And she said she'll pay me. Is it all right with you?"

"You may, as long as you are sure you can handle the responsibility," Mom replied.

"I can," Judy said, hopping up and down with excitement.

A few days later, Judy's best friend, Jill, invited her over for a sleepover. When Judy got home from school, she asked her mom if she could go.

"Aren't you forgetting something?" Mom asked.

Judy looked puzzled. Then a huge frown covered her face. "Oh, no! I forgot about Mrs. Costello's pets! Will you please check on them for me?" Judy asked.

"Judy, it's your responsibility. I'm

not the one who promised to feed them," Mom reminded her.

"But I didn't know Jill was having a sleepover when I agreed to do it. I'm sure I'll be the only one who can't go," Judy grumbled.

"I'd like for you to have fun with your friends, but Mrs. Costello is counting on you," Mom reminded her. "You need to call Jill."

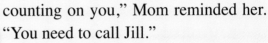

Judy scowled as she went to her room to get her cell phone. "I can't come over," Judy moaned.

"Can't you talk your mom into it? We're going to take pictures and movies of each other with my camera," Jill said.

"I don't think I should ask her again. Why not have the sleepover next weekend so I could be there?" Judy suggested.

"My mom already made plans for my little brother to spend the night with my aunt. You know how he bothers us," Jill replied.

Judy put her phone away and went into the kitchen to fix a snack.

"What are you doing?" Mom asked.

"I'm hungry," Judy said as she peeled a banana and took a bite.

"Mrs. Costello's pets are hungry too," Mom said as she stirred a big pot of soup.

"I'll go right after I eat this," Judy said.

"Mrs. Costello left early this morning, so you need to check on her pets right away," Mom reminded her.

Judy put her banana back on the counter and left for next door. She found the key where Mrs. Costello hid it under the mat and let herself into the house. Bentley, Mrs. Costello's Saint Bernard, met her at the door with sloppy kisses.

"Hi, Bentley. Are you hungry?" Judy scratched Bentley around the ears, then poured dog food into his dish and gave him fresh water. Next, she fed the parrots. Mrs. Costello had told her she didn't need to let them out of their cage until Saturday evening. When she was finished, Judy sat on the floor and brushed Bentley. Bentley leaned against Judy, wiggling this way and that. He looked sad when Judy left.

On Saturday evening, Judy was still unhappy about missing the sleepover. Suddenly, she had an idea. She picked up her cell phone and dialed her friend's number.

"Hi Jill. I'm at Mrs. Costello's. Since I can't come over there, why don't you guys come over here? Besides, I just fed the parrots and let them out of their cage. It's fun watching them fly around the house," Judy said.

A few minutes later, the girls arrived at Mrs. Costello's front door.

"We brought snacks, and we thought it would be fun to fix each other's hair while we're here," Jill announced. She carried two shopping bags. One was full of popcorn, pretzels, and drinks, and the other contained all kinds of hair accessories.

"I'll take the food to the kitchen," Betsy offered, picking up the bag of snacks.

The rest of the girls gathered together in the guest room where there was a large dresser and mirror. "Oh, this is perfect!" Jill exclaimed. "Hey Judy, can I plug in my curling iron over here?"

"Sure," Judy responded as she reached into the bag and pulled out a container full of bright, sparkly hair clips and ponytail holders. The girls giggled and laughed as they began fixing each other's hair. They chatted and ate popcorn while having a fun time experimenting with different hair styles.

"Your turn, Judy," Jill said as she handed her a brush.

Judy pulled her hair up into a ponytail and finished it off with a bright red hair clip that sparkled with glitter.

"Oh, I love that, let's go show Betsy. I bet she's gonna want one in her hair," Judy said as they headed towards the kitchen to find their friend.

The girls ran through the house, laughing and showing off their new hairdos; but it wasn't long before they began to get bored and started looking for something else to do.

"Where are those parrots you were talking about?" Jill asked.

"I don't know. All our noise must have scared them."

The girls began searching each of the rooms until Jill finally yelled out, "Hey, I found them!"

The parrots were in a small tree in the corner of Mrs. Costello's bedroom.

"The female's name is Rose. She's the red one. The green one is Bernie," Judy explained.

Suddenly, Rose flew from the tree to the lamp close to where Judy was standing. Rose turned her head to the side and looked at the bright red clip in Judy's hair. Judy giggled. "I think she likes my new hairdo!" The other girls began to laugh too. Judy bent her head low to give Rose a closer look, but she didn't expect what happened next. Without warning, Rose pecked Judy on the head so hard that she screamed. "Ouch, that hurt!" she cried. "Run! Let's get out of here!"

The girls raced to get out of Mrs. Costello's bedroom. Bentley thought it was great fun to run through the house with the screaming girls and the screeching parrots. The girls grabbed their bag of hair supplies and ran outside.

Judy shut the door and waited outside on the porch while her friends climbed on their bikes and rode away. She knew she had to clean up the snacks they had spilled all over the floor and get the parrots back into their cage. Her head was throbbing. She reached up to touch the place where she had been pecked and was horrified to see a small amount of blood on her hand. She knew she was in big trouble, but she was too afraid to go back inside Mrs. Costello's house. Her heart felt heavy as she ran home.

"Mom, I have a problem," Judy said.

"Are Mrs. Costello's pets all right?" Mom asked.

"They're fine, but I'm not," Judy said, pointing to her injured head.

Judy sat on the sofa and explained what happened while Mom cleaned her wound and applied some medicine. "You are fortunate that this is just a small scratch. It could have been much worse."

"I'm too scared to go back there by myself," Judy confessed.

"I'll come with you," Mom offered. "Parrots are attracted to bright objects like your hair clip and I'm sure they must have been frightened when you girls screamed and ran through the house."

"Thank you for helping me," Judy said after they had cleaned up the scattered food and put the house back in order.

"You shouldn't have invited the girls over to Mrs. Costello's home. She trusted you to care for her pets. She would have been heartbroken if the birds had flown outside or eaten some of the snack food and gotten sick," Mom said. "Jesus wants us to be honest. That means more than just not telling lies. It means keeping promises." ■

Let love and faithfulness never leave you; bind them around your neck, write them on the tablet of your heart. Then you will win favor and a good name in the sight of God and man.
—Proverbs 3:3, 4, NIV

Hanging by a Thread

"**L**ook at that totally awesome tree," Jacob shouted, unable to hide his excitement. I bet I can climb clear to the top!"

If anyone knew whether or not a tree was an awesome climbing tree, it was Jacob. He loved the challenge of climbing as close to the top as possible . . . without breaking a branch!

Jacob and his sister, Shannon, quickly jumped out of the car and ran toward the tree. Moments later, they were weaving their way through the branches, Jacob taking the limb that forked to the left, and Shannon the one to the right.

"Mum, look at me," Shannon waved as she maneuvered herself into a place where a number of branches spread out in different directions and made a perfect seat.

"I see you," Mum waved. "Be careful! Make sure the branch will hold you before you step on it. I wouldn't want you to fall."

"Dad, I love our new home," Jacob

yelled, perched on a branch that was almost as high as the roof of the house.

"But you haven't even been inside yet," his dad replied.

"It doesn't matter what's inside," Jacob called back, "as long as I can have a tree like this in my very own yard!"

A few weeks later, Jacob climbed to the top of the tree where he sat watching the neighbors through a leafy blind, and was on his way down when he decided to try something new. *I bet I could jump directly to the ground from this limb I'm standing on. And if I do fall, the grass will make a soft enough landing. I can do this. No problem!*

Steadying himself, he began to walk to just the right place on the limb where he could launch himself out into space. He studied the ground to find the perfect landing spot and found a thick grassy patch below. He balanced himself on the limb, and then crouched low, ready to spring. Silently he counted to himself . . . *One, two, three, GO.* Then he leaned forward, let go of the branch he was holding on to . . . and jumped!

There was only one problem. There was a small stump left after someone had pruned the tree years before. As Jacob lunged toward the ground, his pants caught on the stump, which flipped him upside down. He began to fall headfirst toward the grassy patch. Quickly, he stretched out his arms to brace himself against the impact. But just before he crashed into the ground . . . he was jolted to an abrupt stop as his pants jerked tight around his hips! *Oh, no! Now what am I going to do?*

Although relieved that he had been spared an almost certain head injury, he was now faced with another dilemma. He was hopelessly caught in the tree. No matter how hard he tried, he could not free himself. He tried to swing far enough to one side to catch a branch with his hands so he could unhook his pants from the stump, but the nearest branch was just out of reach. And he wasn't strong enough to lift his body up to grab the limb closest to him. He was stuck—really stuck!

"Shannon! Shannon! Help!" he screamed at the top of his lungs. *"Shaaaaaaaaanon! Heeeeelp!"*

Shannon was inside putting together a puzzle when she faintly heard her name being called. She came running to see why Jacob was causing such a ruckus. Opening the front door, she took one look at her brother and burst out laughing. There was Jacob hanging upside down from the tree. "What *are* you doing?" she managed to ask between giggles.

"Don't laugh. Just get me down!" Jacob appealed to his little sister. "I'm stuck!"

"Yes, I can see that!" she exclaimed as she laughed even more. But instead of helping her brother out of the tree, she turned around and ran back into the house.

"SHANNON!" Jacob screamed. "Where are you going? I'm stuck, can't you see, you've got to help me!"

MBBS4—4

Ignoring his pleas, she shouted, "Mum, Mum, you've got to see this! Come quick! It's Jacob!"

Mum could tell by the tone of Shannon's voice that something was happening that she shouldn't miss, so she followed Shannon outside, expecting anything but what she saw!

"Mum," Jacob pleaded. "*Pleeeeease* get me down!"

Once Mum determined her son was OK, she couldn't help herself, and joined Shannon who was still laughing hysterically. Then she turned around and went back into the house!

"Mum! Not you too!" Jacob called after her. "I need your help!"

Seconds later Mum returned . . . with a camera!

"Oh, Mum. You aren't serious. Are you really going to take a picture of me in my misery?" Jacob groaned. Starting to see the humor in his predicament, he began to giggle as well.

A few clicks of the camera and much laughter later, Jacob was set free with his feet on the ground. "I can't wait to show Dad those photos," Jacob chuckled. "He's not going to believe it."

As Jacob headed toward the house, he looked over at his awesome climbing tree and smiled as he thought how funny he must have looked hanging upside down. Then his smile faded as he suddenly realized how close he came to landing on his head. "Mum, I could have been hurt really bad. I could have had a serious head injury or even broken my neck and been paralyzed. Jesus must really love me a lot. I think He sent my guardian angel to protect me."

"I think you're right, son. I know we found the humor in it but really we have a lot to praise Jesus for. I can't help thinking about the spiritual lesson here."

"What do you mean, a spiritual lesson?" Jacob asked, curious as to what that could be.

"Well, you were trapped in the tree. There was nothing you could do to get free. And it wasn't until I lifted you up high enough to get your pant leg free from the stump, that you were able to walk away. Because of sin, mankind was trapped with no hope and doomed to die. But just like I came and set you free, Jesus gave His life so that we can be free and live with Him in heaven forever. Jesus loves each of us so much, that He can't imagine heaven without us!" Mum responded giving her son a warm hug.

Jacob thought about what his mother had said. *Wow! Jesus really does love me a lot!* Realizing how God had saved him, He slipped away quietly and knelt by his bed to pray. *Dear Jesus, thank You for sending my guardian angel today. I was hanging by a thread, and You saved me! But thank You most of all for dying on a cross and giving Your life to set us free! I love You, Jesus. Amen.* ■

Looking unto Jesus . . . who for the joy that was set before Him endured the cross, despising the shame, and has sat down at the right hand of the throne of God.
—Hebrews 12:2, NKJV

Blanca's Christmas Wish

A chilling wind whistled around the corners of the tiny wooden house where Blanca lived with her mother, sister, and two brothers in Reynosa, Mexico. Winter had arrived! While no snow fell in this part of Mexico, bitter wintry blasts blew hard from the north.

"Brrrr!" Blanca shivered and snuggled deeper under the heavy red, yellow, and green woolen blanket on her small cot. She tucked the edge under her chin.

"I really don't like winter! It's too cold," her younger sister, Rena, complained.

"I like it," Blanca admitted. "It means Christmas is coming." Blanca closed her eyes and imagined the portable radio she wanted her mother to give her for Christmas.

Christmas in Blanca's home didn't include a brightly decorated Christmas tree, strings of lights, or stockings hanging from the fireplace. Blanca's mother couldn't afford such things.

There weren't even any pictures on the orange stucco walls of their house.

But Blanca's home wasn't any poorer than those of her friends. No one in the neighborhood owned a television set, a stereo, or video games. They didn't even have an indoor bathroom or running water.

To take a bath, Blanca would drag a metal washtub to the front yard and fill it half full of cold water

from the outdoor spigot next to the house. Then she would ask one of her older brothers to help her drag the tub inside the house where she would scoop up the cold water with a bowl and dump it over herself, scrub up with a bar of soap, and then rinse off the soap with more cold water.

In the summer, the cold water felt good. But in the winter, Blanca shivered from the frigid bath water. She didn't complain, however, for she knew her mother was doing the best she could to clothe and feed her children.

Blanca loved school and playing soccer with her neighborhood friends. But on the weekends, the thing she loved best was attending church with Marcie, her missionary friend, where she would hear stories and sing songs about how much Jesus loves her. She also learned about the Ten Commandments—including the one about honoring her parents—and she was always happier when she did what the Bible said.

After school each day, and on weekends when she wasn't in church, Blanca helped her mother sell tacos at a tiny stand on a busy street in town. Mama called Blanca her *little gopher*. Blanca's job was to *go for this* and to *go for that*. Each day, Blanca went to the mill to buy the corn flour her mother used to make the tortillas. She also kept the red and white chest filled with ice to keep the cans of soda cold for Mama's customers.

With Christmas coming, Blanca knew that Mama would buy her a

special gift. What Blanca wanted more than anything else in the world was a wind-up radio that didn't need batteries or electricity to operate. She had seen such a radio in the window of Martinez's gift shop. Blanca imagined herself falling asleep each night to the music of Mexico City's best mariachi bands.

On Christmas Eve, Mama closed the taco stand early and came home to fix a big supper for the entire family, including her aunts, uncles, cousins, and grandparents. Every year, as Mama shaped the Christmas tamales, she always said, "We might not be able to fill our home with lots of Christmas presents, but we certainly can fill it with lots of love."

Mama's hands were coated in corn flour when there was a knock at the front door. "Blanca, can you please answer that?"

Blanca instantly obeyed. It was Marcie, who was carrying a large cardboard box. "My sister in the United States sent me a big box of clothing and I can't use everything, so I was thinking that maybe there are some things in here that your family could wear," she explained.

Blanca shot a hopeful glance toward her mother. "How very nice of you to think of us," Mama told Marcie.

Inside the box, Blanca found a pair of blue jeans for each of her brothers, a pink and yellow dress for Rena, and there was a pair of jeans that looked to be about her size at the bottom of the box. Blanca squealed with delight, then held them up to her tall slender body.

"I think they'll fit just fine,"

Photo taken by: Lichelle Olivera

Mama commented. "Why don't you try them on?"

It took Blanca no time at all to run into her room, slip out of her faded red skirt, and into the blue jeans. Each of the excited children modeled their new clothes from their generous friend. As Marcie was leaving, Blanca rushed to give her a big hug and an extra "thank you" for the surprise gifts.

Blanca changed back into her skirt and hurried to the kitchen to help her mother cook the tamales for supper. By the time the family began to arrive, the kitchen smelled of freshly made burritos, hot tamales, and Blanca's favorite, taco soup.

Throughout the evening meal, which seemed to go on forever, Blanca eyed the small stack of packages her mother had wrapped in plain brown paper. Finally, the moment arrived for Blanca to open her present. But when Blanca squeezed her package, her heart sank. The package was soft, not hard like a radio would be.

As she removed the last layer of paper, a green sweater fell into her lap. She tried to smile, but tears welled up in her eyes. A lump filled her throat. *I can't cry,* she thought. *What would everyone think?*

Photo taken by: Lichelle Olivera

"Thank you, Mama." Blanca pressed her lips against her mother's cheek.

Mama didn't miss the disappointment in her daughter's eyes. "I know how much you love green. And I knew you needed something to keep you warm this winter. You're growing so fast. I wish I could do more."

"That's OK, Mama. Thank you for the sweater." Blanca slipped away from the family circle and ran to her room to cry.

She was angry. She had worked so hard to please her mother. And Mama knew how much Blanca wanted a radio.

Sometimes it doesn't pay to be good, Blanca sniffed back her tears.

I tried to help Mama. I did everything she asked and all I get for my hard work is a dumb green sweater. But, as soon as that ugly thought came into her mind, she instantly felt bad. Blanca liked helping Mama at the taco stand because she loved her mother, not because Mama might buy her a radio.

After a short time, Blanca wiped her tears on her pillowcase, combed her hair, and joined the family in time to hear her favorite uncle play some old Mexican folk songs on his guitar.

Overnight, the weather turned bitterly cold, almost cold enough to snow. Blanca awoke to the sound of her mother humming in the kitchen. She shivered as she dragged herself out of her warm bed.

Blanca smiled. Today was Christmas and Mama would not be selling tacos. That would mean that Blanca would be able to spend some time with her friends. As she rubbed her arms to warm them, Blanca spotted her disappointing Christmas gift—the green sweater draped over the back of her bedroom chair. She sighed as she reluctantly pulled the sweater over her head and slipped her arms into the sleeves. *At least it will keep me warm at the taco stand,* she thought. Blanca tugged the sweater into place. It fit perfectly. Then it dawned on her. *Hey, I can wear the sweater with my new blue jeans.*

After helping her mother wash the breakfast dishes, Blanca hurried outside to find her friends. Regardless of the sun shining in the sky, the cold winds continued to whip around the buildings, stirring up dust as they blew.

"Hey, Blanca, nice sweater!" Her best friend, Eva, ran toward her from across the street. She reached out and touched Blanca's arm. "Oh, it's so soft."

"It's warm too," said Blanca with a cheery smile. "Mama gave it to me for Christmas."

Blanca realized, for the first time in days, that she wasn't cold. The sweater kept her so warm that when she prepared for bed, she briefly considered sleeping in it, but quickly changed her mind. She wanted her new sweater to stay nice for as long as possible.

Maybe someday, Blanca reasoned as she carefully folded the sweater, *I'll own a portable radio; but for now, this sweater is what I really need. Mama loves me and was thinking about keeping me warm when she bought it.*

Photo taken by: Haziel Olivera

All winter long, whenever the cold winds blew, Blanca wore her soft green sweater and thanked God for such a special Mama who gave her the best Christmas gift of all . . . a gift of love! ■

And my God shall supply all your need according to His riches in glory by Christ Jesus.
—Philippians 4:19, NKJV

Play Ball

Garrett and Griffin scanned the list posted on the bulletin board. They had worked hard all spring hoping to make the Coldwater Colts, the baseball league's elite team. Only the best made it . . . and, this year, they hoped it would include them.

"Yes!" Griffin pumped his hand into the air as he saw his name printed about halfway down the list. His twin brother, Garrett, pushed passed him, looking over the list. And there, at the very bottom, was his name too.

"Yeah!" Garrett bumped fists with his twin. "We both made it!"

"Can't imagine doing it without you." Griffin smiled at his brother. They always did everything together.

Griffin glanced again at the notice. On the bottom was a note from the coach. He got up close to read the fine print. It read, "An additional tryout for pitcher will be held next Wednesday immediately after school."

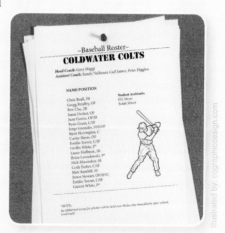

"Wow, there's another tryout next week," Griffin announced. "That's when the coach decides who will be the starting pitcher."

"Are you going to try out?" Garrett watched while his twin read the notice again. They both loved to pitch. Now they had to decide what would happen if they both tried out and one of them actually got the starting position.

"You really want it, don't you?" Griffin knew his brother well.

"Yeah. But you do too." Garrett looked like he was thinking. "I say we both try out and see what happens. We'll pray about it and see where God leads. Maybe neither one of us will get it. It's just great that we both made the team, right?"

Griffin knew Garrett really wanted to pitch this year. Garrett had played second base in the past seasons, while Griffin was often the starting pitcher. *Maybe I should back down this time*, he thought. *But this is the the league's best team. It sure would be fun to pitch again this year.*

The twins practiced hard. Sometimes they took turns pitching to each other. And sometimes they practiced side by side, throwing their best pitches into the mitts of their friends.

Garrett's arm was looking stronger and stronger. Maybe he had a chance to win the coveted position. Garrett kept praying about it, asking God to help him accept whatever happened.

Griffin watched as his brother got better, throwing curveballs like a pro. *How would I feel if Garrett gets to be starting pitcher instead of me?* he wondered. *It might hurt my pride losing to my own brother. What would my friends think?* Griffin prayed that God would help him accept the fact that having a winning team was more important than who was chosen to be pitcher.

On tryout day, five guys ran out to the field as soon as school was over. They were warming up their arms and stretching their bodies in hopes of showing the coach that they were the perfect choice to be the starting pitcher. The bleachers were soon filled with excited parents as the tryouts began.

Griffin walked nervously to the mound to pitch first. Each player would get to throw for one inning in a mock game. Griffin struck out two of the batters. That made him feel pretty good. His team held the scoring to only one run while he was pitching.

Two other guys showed their stuff before it was Garrett's turn. Garrett had rooted for all the tryouts from his position on second base. "Way to go, Griffin." "Great throw, Matt." "That's a great arm, Jordan." He decided it didn't matter who got the position, because they were going to work together as a team, and that's what mattered most. Garrett stepped on to the pitcher's mound and scooted the toe of his foot around in the dirt. He took a second to pray — not that he would win, but that he would do his very best. Then, nothing else would matter.

"Batter up!" the umpire called from his position behind the catcher.

Eric stepped up to the plate. Garrett grimaced. Eric was a left-handed batter. He wasn't as good throwing for lefties. He took his time and tried to think about each pitch. The first flew over the base a little low.

"Ball," the umpire called.

Garrett took a deep breath and let loose a fastball. It flew over the plate, right in the middle of the strike zone. Eric didn't even swing at it.

"Strike."

Two balls and another strike crossed the plate. Garrett knew that his next pitch would have to be right on target. He wound up, threw the ball, and watched it slowly sail to the plate. Eric swung at it, but, at the last second, the ball dropped and he missed.

"Out!" the umpire yelled.

Everyone in the bleachers cheered.

Garrett struck out the next batter too. The third ended up walking to first base. The next batter popped up a fly ball and Garrett ran from the mound to catch it. That was it, three outs. He was done.

"You did great," Griffin called as he ran out to meet his twin. "That's the best pitching I've ever seen you do."

"We worked well together. That's what matters." Garrett grinned at his teammates.

The coach wrote something on his notepad, then called the last guy to the mound.

That night was a long night in the Bailey home. The twins knew the starting position could go to any of the guys. They had all done well. Garrett studied quietly in his bedroom while Griffin looked at his baseball cards, imagining maybe one day his picture would be on a rookie card too.

The list of the chosen players and their positions wouldn't be posted until after school. As soon as the last bell rang, everyone ran to see the results.

"Here they come," someone shouted. The crowd around the bulletin board parted, and the twins looked at each other. Both felt nervous inside.

Griffin saw his name first. He then looked for Garrett's name on the roster. It wasn't listed next to second base where it usually was. It was now listed at the bottom, in the spot where his name had always been. Garrett was the new pitcher. He turned slowly to look at his brother.

"Congratulations, Garrett." He meant it. He really did. But he had to admit it hurt. He wasn't the starting pitcher this year. Instead, it was his brother, his best friend in all the world!

"I can't believe it." Garrett marveled as he read the list.

"You deserve it. You've worked hard."

"We all have. What a great team we'll be, right?"

Griffin struggled, but not for long. He had a choice to make. He could be thankful that he was on the very best team, no matter what position he played. Or he could be jealous of his twin. But where would that get him? He had been a starting pitcher, and now he would have his turn playing second base. At least he would have a good look at his brother as he led their team to victory.

Griffin raised his arm and held up his fist to his twin. Garrett bounced his knuckles off of his brother's. "For the team!" Griffin shouted. It was going to be a winning season, in more ways than one. ■

Rejoice with those who rejoice.
—Romans 12:15, NKJV

The Butterfly Pin

It was summer and Emily was bored. "There's nothing to do around here," Emily complained to her mom. "And I'm tired of having to entertain Amanda. All she wants to do is play with me."

"Well," said her mom, "Amanda looks up to you. After all, you are her big sister and she thinks you are pretty special. In her eyes, you can do no wrong. So, it's no wonder she wants to be with you all the time."

"I know," said Emily. "I just wish we could do something different this summer."

A couple of weeks later, Dad's office manager had to leave town suddenly because of a family emergency and would be gone for three weeks. Dad was desperate. Mom was the only person he knew who could do the job without training.

"So, honey, do you think you can find someone to take care of the girls for three weeks, or should I start interviewing and hire a temp?"

"Emily's been complaining that she's bored, so I've been thinking maybe we should send her to day camp. I could call and ask if Amanda's old enough to go with her. I think the girls would enjoy doing something different."

And so it was arranged. The next day, when Mom dropped the girls off at Wapato Lake Day Camp, they were met by Mrs. Turner and her assistant, Lynette. After they registered, the girls joined a game of kickball. There were so many activities that the morning went quickly. After lunch, Lynette announced they would all be at the craft center making pins that they could wear on their jackets or dresses.

"Girls, the first thing you need to do is find a picture that you would like on your pin." There was a scramble for pictures as the girls tried to find one they liked best. There were pictures of dogs, kittens, birds, and flowers. There were squeals of delight as each girl settled on the picture she wanted.

"Amanda, look at the kitten I found. Isn't he cute? This picture will make a really nice pin."

Amanda nodded her head and continued her own search for the perfect picture.

Emily carefully cut out the picture of her kitten. Next, she oiled her mold and placed the kitten picture face down. She then mixed and stirred the plaster and poured it into the mold. Lynette told her to tap the mold gently to remove any air bubbles and then continue to fill her mold to the top. To finish, she placed a fastener into the plaster, just deep enough to hold it.

Lynette called to the girls as she stood at the door, "Let's go sing some camp songs while we wait for the pins to dry." Since Emily really liked Lynette, she hurried to catch up with her so they could spend some time together.

Singing camp songs was fun, but Emily was anxious to get back to see how her pin had turned out. When they returned to the craft center, the girls were instructed on how to take their pins out of the molds and then gently sand any rough edges. Next, Lynette sprayed each of the pins with a glossy finish, which would make them look shiny.

When all the pins had been placed on the table, Emily spotted the most beautiful pin she had ever seen. It was a colorful butterfly with brilliant shades of blue. Never in all her life had Emily wanted anything so badly as she wanted that pin. She picked it up for a closer look.

A voice startled her. "Do you like my pin, Emily?"

Emily looked up into the smiling face of Lynette.

"Oh, er—ah—yes, I do," Emily replied, completely flustered.

A few minutes later, Lynette went outside to watch some girls practicing cartwheels, leaving Emily alone at the table. She stood there for a few minutes, admiring all the pins. The butterfly pin was by far the prettiest. Oh, how she wanted that pin. She picked it up again and looked around. No one was watching. But wait. What was it she had learned in Bible class at church last week? *Jesus sees everything*. She quickly brushed that thought aside. She took one more look at the lovely butterfly pin, slipped it into her pocket, and walked away.

Somehow after that, camp just wasn't as much fun. The butterfly pin was like a heavy weight in her pocket and her conscience bothered her too. Her mind seemed to say, *You really shouldn't have taken Lynette's*

MBBS4—5

pin. Stealing is a sin! Again, Emily pushed the thought from her mind.

At the end of the day, Mrs. Turner blew the whistle for the girls to sit under the shade trees to wait for their parents to pick them up. Then she reminded the older girls to be sure to pick up their pins before leaving.

Back at the tables, Emily heard Lynette say, "My pin is gone! It had a beautiful butterfly on it. I left it right here. What could have happened to it?"

Emily felt even worse now, but she pulled herself together. She had to act innocent. She sat down next to Amanda. "Aren't you going to get your pin?" Amanda asked.

"I already got it," Emily whispered and changed the subject.

Mrs. Turner gathered all the girls together for a final goodbye and asked, "Girls, Lynette made a butterfly pin and it's missing. Do any of you know what might have happened to it?"

No one said anything. Emily's forehead got all sweaty and her cheeks turned red, but she shook her head *No* along with all the other girls.

By the time Mom drove up, Emily was feeling so guilty that she couldn't even look at Lynette when she said goodbye.

In the car, Amanda was bubbling over with joy as she told her mom all the wonderful things she had done at day camp. Emily, however, was strangely quiet.

"Did you have a good time?" Mom asked Emily.

"Yes," Emily replied.

"Well, I've heard all about Amanda's day. So, tell me, what did you do?"

"Played."

"Is that all?" Mom asked.

"Show her the kitten pin you made," Amanda said. "It's really neat!"

"It's nothing." Emily tried to sound like it wasn't important.

"Come on," Amanda insisted.

Finally, Emily pulled the butterfly pin out of her pocket.

"Emily!" Amanda was shocked. "That's not your pin. That's the one Lynette made."

By this time, tears were streaming down Emily's face.

Mom pulled the car over under a shady tree and turned off the engine. "Honey, do you want to tell me what happened?"

The entire story spilled out.

"Emily, I can't believe you stole that," Amanda said as she shook her head.

"I can't believe I did it either," confessed Emily. "I'm so embarrassed. What will Lynette think of me when she learns the truth?"

"Well, I know one thing," Mom said. "The longer you wait to tell her, the harder it will be. I think we should turn around right now so you can return the pin and tell Lynette how sorry you are for taking it." And that's exactly what they did.

That night, Emily's thoughts went back over the events of the day. She had made it right with everyone else and now it was time to make it right with Jesus. She knelt beside her bed and prayed, "Dear Jesus, I know You saw me take the butterfly pin. I'm so sorry. Please forgive me for stealing and then lying about it. I disappointed everyone today: You, Amanda, Lynette, Mom and Dad . . . and myself. I am so, so sorry. Help me to be good. Help me to be more like You. Amen." ■

> *Treasures of wickedness profit nothing,*
> *But righteousness delivers from death.*
> —Proverbs 10:2, NKJV

Broken Windshield

Summer vacation had begun only two weeks ago and already Craig was bored. Throughout the school year Craig had daydreamed of no more homework or early morning bus rides. He saw himself enjoying the warm summer months: sleeping in, lazing about in front of the TV, and enjoying baseball games and pool parties organized by his family's apartment complex. But now that summer was here, things weren't quite as fun as he had imagined.

He grew tired of lazing around the house. And, despite his valiant efforts to organize games or go to the pool, all of his friends were out of town, sick, or away at camp. He lay on his bed, staring into space and wondered what to do. He didn't have any siblings to pester, no pets to care for, and his parents were at work most of the day.

Not knowing what to do, he decided to go outside on the deck of their second-floor apartment. *At least I'll get some fresh air,* he thought.

Craig opened the sliding glass door and was greeted with a warm, balmy breeze. Shutting the door behind him, he took a seat on one of the gray weather-beaten plastic chairs and enjoyed the view . . . of the parking lot. Lovely. He considered how full the parking lot was, and yet, how everyone he knew was unavailable. Just beyond the parking lot was the large grassy commons area where games were played. In the corner of the deck, he noticed his mother's latest attempt at gardening—an almost dead fern trying to grow in a large pot surrounded by decorative stones.

Craig picked up one of the stones and absentmindedly rubbed his thumb over its smooth, flat surface. It would make a great skipping rock if there were any water around. Then an idea struck him. Looking at the green commons area and then at the full parking lot, he wondered just how far he could throw a rock. Could he throw it over the cars and hit the grass?

Standing up by the edge of the railing, he reared back and flung the stone as hard as he could. It made a lovely arc and sailed over the sea of cars, landing safely in the soft grass of the commons. He was rather impressed with himself. Grabbing another stone, he launched it into the air with the same results.

After several satisfying throws, he wondered how close to the cars he could get and still have the stone land in the field. He sifted through the remaining stones in the fern's pot and settled on a flat, gray one. Smooth and light, he had no doubt he could skim it over the tops of the vehicles.

Carefully eyeing his target—a black Ford Thunderbird and the edge of grass just beyond—he wound up and threw. The stone left his hand like a bullet. He watched it drop and held his breath. The stone—whirling

around and around at an incredible speed—found its mark. It landed, not in the grass . . . but instead, shot right through the windshield of that black Thunderbird just like a speeding bullet!

It left a small hole surrounded by shattered glass. Craig felt his heart leap into his throat. Quickly, he ducked down and looked around to see if anyone had witnessed what he had done. There was no one in sight.

Carefully, he stepped back inside the apartment and sat down on the couch. His stomach felt queasy. *OK, just think for a second. No one saw me. I'm just fine. Just be calm. But, if the car was parked outside, it could mean the owner is inside this apartment building! What if they saw the rock fly through the air while they sat on their deck? They'll probably call the police and there will be a knock on my door any second!* A fretful hour passed.

Convincing himself that all was well, he watched some television, ate a snack, and tried to read a book until his parents got home. When they arrived, Craig spoke very little. Wanting an excuse to go to his room, he mumbled something to them about not feeling well. Both his parents exchanged worried glances.

After twenty minutes or so, his dad came in and checked on him. "Craig," he said, "how are you feeling?"

"My stomach hurts," he replied, and turned over on his side—away from his father's gaze.

"I'm sorry, son. Do you think it's something you ate?"

Craig just grunted.

"Well, if you're not feeling any better soon, let us know." Then his father left.

Craig got up and sat on the edge of his bed. The way Dad looked at him made him wonder. *Do they know what I did? If they do, why don't they just say something?*

Another twenty minutes passed, and Mom came into the room. "Hey honey," she said, sitting next to him on the bed and placing a hand on his forehead. "Feel any better?" He felt worse. He couldn't stop thinking about that broken windshield.

"Not really," he muttered.

His mom gave him a thoughtful look. "Let me know if there's anything I can do."

He thanked her and watched her leave the room. *Why are my parents acting like this? They must know about the windshield.*

Finally, Craig couldn't stand it any longer. *It's hopeless,* he thought. *This won't go away until I tell them.* He closed his eyes and said a brief prayer, asking God for mercy and to help him survive whatever punishment they gave him. Getting up, he made his way out to the living room. His parents were sitting on the couch. Mom was reading the paper and Dad was working on his laptop.

"Hey, sport," his dad said, "feeling better?"

"Well," began Craig, "not really, and I'll probably feel worse after I tell you what's wrong." Mom put her paper down to give him her full attention. She wore a concerned expression and reassured him that they would help him with  whatever trouble he was in. Fighting off tears, Craig confessed the whole boredom-induced incident that resulted in the broken windshield. Once he was finished, his parents gave him a hug.

"We knew all about it," they said.

Pulling away, Craig looked surprised. "You did? But how?"

They gave him a weird smile—not the response he expected. "You forgot to close the sliding glass door," Mom said. "When I went to close it, I saw the stones in the fern pot had been rummaged through and some were scattered on the deck. I looked up and saw the broken windshield. That's how I figured it out."

His dad stood and placed a hand on his shoulder. "We're glad you have a healthy conscience and told us the truth."

"How much trouble am I in?" Craig asked with a look of concern.

"Well, first you're going to have to tell Mr. Braddock what happened  to his Thunderbird. He lives right down the hallway in apartment 320. And, of course, you will be using your allowance to reimburse him for the expense of getting the windshield fixed. But apart from that, I think you have punished yourself enough. The consequence of making it right is enough for you to learn a valuable lesson about the importance of making good decisions and taking responsibility for mistakes."

Craig was glad there wouldn't be any grounding or taking away of privileges, but he dreaded the confrontation with Mr. Braddock. It took him most of the evening to work up the nerve to visit apartment 320.

He knocked three times on the door and, for a moment, thought no one would answer. But the lock on the other side rattled and Mr. Braddock opened the door. "Hello, may I help you?" he asked.

Craig stammered as he introduced himself. Then the whole story of the broken windshield came pouring out. "Of course," Craig said, "I'll pay to get it fixed."

Mr. Braddock looked surprised as Craig confessed what he had done. Craig braced for a scolding, but instead the man smiled and shook his hand warmly.

"Thank you, young man," he said. "I was laid off from work today, and finances are really tight. I have been fretting about the broken windshield ever since I discovered it this afternoon. Thank you for being honest and for being willing to pay for the damages," he said warmly.

Photo taken by: cagraphicdesign.com

That night before going to bed, Craig reflected on all that had happened. Trying to keep his actions secret caused so much anxiety, while a simple confession felt so good. The consequences would be costly, but it was a small price to pay for a clean conscience . . . and a good night's sleep. ■

Finally, I confessed all my sins to you and stopped trying to hide my guilt. . . . And you forgave me! All my guilt is gone.
—Psalm 32:5, NLT

One Sister Too Many

"**E**llie!" Ashlee hissed. "Go away and leave us alone!"

Ashlee and Lauren both glared at little Ellie. She glared back at them. "I'm telling my mom."

As Ellie jumped up to run back to the other picnic table, Lauren stuck her tongue out at her. "She's getting to be a real pest," Lauren said to her sister. "We don't really have to play with her, do we?"

Ashlee frowned. "Dad will say that we do. I wish he hadn't gotten married again. We didn't need a little sister. That makes one sister too many."

Lauren agreed. "I wish we were at Mom's house this weekend." They both watched while Ellie ran up to the woman sitting beside their dad.

Ashlee saw her dad smile at Ellie and pat her head. His smile grew even bigger when he looked at Ellie's mom. "But it is good to see Dad happy again. Ellie's mom is OK . . . I guess. And Ellie is just, well . . . she's just six years old. And that's really annoying."

They both watched as their dad got up from the picnic table and walked over to them. Ellie followed a little way behind him. "Ashlee, Lauren, what's the matter? Why won't you play with Ellie? I know she's younger than you two and I know you sometimes feel she's a pest. But she's your sister now. She's part of our family."

"Dad, we're trying to play a game," Ashlee said. "Ellie's not old enough to understand the rules. She always does it wrong."

"No, I don't," Ellie insisted.

Dad sighed. "Well, at least let her watch."

"Sure, Dad," Ashlee said sweetly.

As their father left, Ashlee and Lauren turned their backs on Ellie and started playing their game again. "Your turn, Lauren," Ashlee said.

"I *do* know the rules," Ellie said. "Lauren got a three, and she gets to go three spaces."

Lauren ignored her. "I rolled a three," she said to Ashlee with a wink. "Now I have to go backwards four spaces—because it's after lunch."

Ellie shook her head. They still ignored her. "And I rolled a two," Ashlee said next. "So I have to go forward six spaces—one for each letter of my name."

"That's not how you play!" Ellie cried. She tried to tell them what to do, but they just pretended she wasn't there. Finally, she stomped away.

"That'll teach her," Lauren said with a smile. "Maybe she won't try to hang around us all the time now. Come on, let's start over and play the game the right way."

Before long, their dad was back. This time he looked unhappy with them. "I expect you girls to play with Ellie nicely," he said, looking straight at Ashlee and Lauren.

"OK, Dad. We will," Ashlee replied. "I have an idea," she whispered to Lauren as he walked away. "Let's pretend we want to go exploring in the woods with Ellie. Then we'll hide from her and she'll think she's lost."

"That's a great idea," Lauren whispered back. "Maybe if she gets scared, she won't want to play with us anymore."

Ashlee called out, "Ellie, do you want to go exploring with us?"

"Can I?" Ellie asked as she came running over. "That would be fun."

The three girls headed down a path into the woods. They wandered down one trail after another. Finally, Ashlee stopped beside a big stump. "You guys wait here," she said. "I'm going to see what's behind those trees."

After a minute, Lauren said, "I'll go see what Ashlee's doing. You wait here." Then she ran after Ashlee, leaving Ellie all alone.

"*Psst!* Lauren! Over here!" Ashlee waved to Lauren from behind some bushes. "Is Ellie following you?"

Lauren crawled in beside her. "I didn't see her coming, but I'm sure she will be in a minute. She's probably scared already."

The two of them sat there quietly. They heard birds chirping overhead. They heard insects buzzing through the leaves. But they didn't hear a sound from Ellie.

"Where is she?" Ashlee whispered. "She should be running after you by now, shouting or crying. We've been here for a long time." Suddenly, Ashlee's eyes got big. "What if something happened to her?"

The same thought hit Lauren. "You don't think she's hurt or anything, do you? I didn't want to hurt her. I didn't think . . . "

"We didn't think at all," Ashlee interrupted, pushing her way out of the bushes. "She's just a little kid. Come on!"

They both ran back up the path. "Ellie! Ellie! Where are you?"

But Ellie didn't answer. When they ran up to the big stump, Ellie was gone.

"Oh, no," Lauren panted. "She's gone! She really is lost!"

Ashlee's eyes filled with tears. "She can't be gone. We have to find her! Oh, Lauren, how could we be so mean? She just wants someone to play with. She hasn't always had a sister like we have."

"We left her alone in the woods instead of protecting her." Lauren slumped to the ground. "What are we going to do?"

"We're going to pray," Ashlee said, dropping to her knees. "We're going to ask God to keep Ellie safe and to help us find her." Ashlee closed her eyes. "Dear Jesus, we're sorry we tried to trick Ellie. Please keep her safe."

"And God," Lauren added, "I promise to change and be a better sister. Please help us find her! Thank You, Jesus. Amen"

They hopped up from their knees. "I'll go down this path," Ashlee said, pointing left, "and you go that way. Shout if you find her."

Ashlee ran as fast as she could over the bumpy path, calling, "Ellie! Ellie! Can you hear me?" She dashed up to the edge of a stream and almost fell in. Before she could jump across, she heard a sound.

"*Shhh!*" There, beside a tree trunk, was Ellie. "*Shhh,*" she said again. "You're going to scare the bunny." Ellie pointed across the stream to where a rabbit sat with its nose quivering. "I followed him all the way here."

Just then, the rabbit disappeared down a hole.

"*Awww,* Ashlee, you scared it away."

"Ellie, are you OK? I thought you were lost!" Then she remembered Lauren. "Lauren!" Ashlee shouted. "Lauren! Over here!"

Ashlee then knelt down by her new little sister. "Ellie, I'm sorry I've been mean to you. I'm glad you're OK." Silently, she added, *Thank You, God, for keeping her safe.*

"Come on, Ellie," she said, hopping up. "Let's go find Lauren."

"Will she help us find another bunny?" Ellie asked.

"I'm sure she will. That's what big sisters are for!" ■

How good and pleasant it is when brothers [sisters] live together in unity!
—Psalm 133:1, NIV

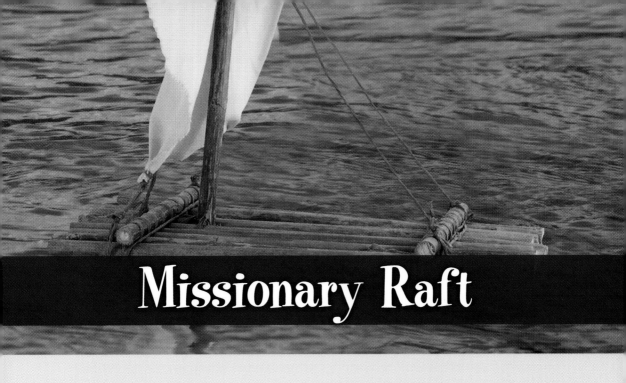

Missionary Raft

Charlie looked out the window and watched heavy raindrops splash on the stone walkway leading to his home. Clouds hung dark and gloomy above the trees as every once in a while a flicker of lightning would illuminate the leaves, causing them to shimmer for a moment, then fade back into shadows. This was not exactly the type of day he had hoped for.

With a sigh, Charlie turned from the window and sat down heavily on his bed. *It sure rains a lot here,* he thought to himself, *especially when I've got something very important to do.*

That "something very important" sat resting on his dresser. Charlie stood and walked over to it, admiring its carefully constructed lines and sturdy appearance. It was the best sailing raft he had ever built—and he had built his share of sailing rafts. But this one was special. This one was made from heavier bamboo and the lashings holding everything together

were leather shoelaces taken—with permission—from his dad's old work boots.

He picked up his creation and held it at arm's length. *Just look at that mast—straight and tall, complete with handkerchief sail ready to harvest the winds and send this little craft skimming over the waves!* He had even remembered to include a rudder so the raft would head in the direction he had chosen for it to go. *Yes, it is a fine piece of workmanship.* But right now, the problem wasn't finding water on which to sail it. The problem was that there was too much water falling from the sky and Mom had made it quite clear that he couldn't sail his new raft until the storm passed. So Charlie returned to his bed and plunked himself down with another sigh. He would wait, even though he would rather not.

Being a missionary and living in a country where everyone spoke a language that sounded strange to his ears never really bothered him. As a matter of fact, he had visited the United States—where his mother and father were born—only once in his life. It was OK. But now, he was back in Singapore where his dad worked at the mission office just across the street and down the hill from his home. Actually, this country seemed more like where he belonged.

Once, Charlie had asked his dad, "What exactly does a missionary do?" He figured he should know since he was one. Dad had simply stated, "A missionary tells people about God's love." He had seen his father do just that—preach in big auditoriums and speak in various churches throughout the country. Charlie figured that someday he would learn to tell people about God too.

In time, Charlie noticed that the trees outside his window seemed a little brighter. As a matter of fact, the sound of falling rain had softened from a roar to a quiet whisper. It was over. IT WAS OVER! The storm was moving on, leaving the world washed clean and bright.

Grabbing his raft from the dresser, Charlie hurried through the house, his bare feet stomping on the wooden floors. "I'm going outside now," he called to his mother who was ironing clothes. "Rain's gone."

Mother smiled and glanced out the window. "Don't wander off too far," she called. "Supper's in an hour."

The warm, moist air felt good to Charlie's bare arms and legs as he splashed through the puddles in front of his house. Beside the road was a ditch into which the newly fallen rain was collecting and being sent down the hill where it finally left the mission compound. The ditch formed the "river" and the spots where water was backed up onto the lawns created beautiful "oceans" for serious rafting.

Choosing a spot where the water wasn't running too quickly, Charlie knelt and placed his bamboo creation on the surface and watched as gentle breezes billowed the handkerchief sail. Immediately, the little craft moved out away from the shore just like the sailboats in the port of Singapore. It was working! The rudder was keeping the raft on course as the white sail moved it over the water.

That's when things started to happen in a hurry. The current under the raft began moving faster and faster, carrying the little craft along with it. Charlie stood up quickly, a worried look clouding his face. This wasn't good. Already his vessel was too far out in the rushing water to be reached by his arms, his big toe, or even a stick.

He ran along the road, trying to keep the raft in sight as it bobbed and weaved its way under bushes, around boulders, through cement culverts passing under driveways, and along rows of parked cars. Faster and faster,

MBBS4—6

it went. Faster and faster, Charlie ran, splashing through puddles, jumping over obstacles, stumbling through underbrush, and, finally, hurrying right out through the open gates of the mission compound and into the big world beyond.

Then . . . the raft was gone. All he saw was water—rushing, bouncing, bubbling waves of churning water running here and there among rows of simple bamboo and grass houses and over mud-clogged streets. His work, his careful designing, his dream of building the perfect bamboo raft had vanished, lost in the wet world left by the storm. He reluctantly walked home with his head down, feeling very defeated by the events that had just taken place.

The next day, Charlie returned to the village outside the mission compound in search of his lost creation. The muddy streets and wind-

blown houses now baked in the bright sunlight as people moved through the shadows and chickens clucked and scratched for food under the bushes.

Charlie was hoping that his bamboo raft had survived the churning waters and would be found lodged under a piece of wood or perhaps left high and dry on some vacant plot of land. He heard some children laughing and splashing down the street and headed in their direction. Maybe they had seen his raft. Maybe they could help him search.

As he approached them, Charlie stopped suddenly. What he saw caused his breath to catch in his throat. There, amid the tanned legs and feet of three children, floated a perfectly constructed bamboo raft, complete with a tall mast and billowing handkerchief sail. The little girl in the group was kneeling in the puddle and blowing air into the sail, causing the craft to move majestically over the waves as her friends squealed in delight.

Then, her companion would adjust the rudder and blow the raft in the opposite direction as the third playmate stirred the waters with his feet. Charlie wished he could understand what they were saying. But it was obvious the children were overjoyed to be playing with his raft.

In fact, the three were having so much fun that they didn't even notice the missionary boy with the fair skin and wondering eyes watching them. They continued to play together, lost in the wonderful world of imagination and joy.

When the girl finally glanced in Charlie's direction, she stood quickly to her feet. Her companions did the same. Slowly, realization crept into her mind. The raft . . . it had a designer, a builder, an owner, and he was standing on the other side of the muddy street watching her.

Wordlessly, she pointed at the craft and then at Charlie as a sad smile creased her mud-caked face. Then she waited to see how the visitor would respond.

Charlie frowned slightly. It was his raft. It was the result of his hard work and creativity. But he knew that in all the hours he would play with it, it would never bring so much laughter and so much joy as he was seeing in the faces and hearing in the voices of those children.

Charlie lifted his hand and pointed at the raft. Then he nodded his head and waved at the little girl. He had a big smile on his face as he turned and walked away.

As he re-entered the gates of the mission compound, he could hear distant laughter as three children played in the puddles in front of their simple home. That's when Charlie understood that sometimes you can be a missionary without saying a word. ■

Each man should give what he has decided in his heart to give, not reluctantly or under compulsion, for God loves a cheerful giver.
—2 Corinthians 9:7, NIV

Gina Goes to Jail

It was Sunday morning—the day Mom always bought an extra thick newspaper, clipped coupons, and checked the sales. Mom usually rode her bicycle four or five miles on Sunday and would stop by the local convenience store on her way home to pick up the paper. But today, she wasn't feeling well, so had decided to forgo the biking.

"Gina, would you mind going to the store to buy a newspaper for me?"

"Sure, Mom, how soon do you need it?"

"I'd actually like it as soon as possible, if you're not in the middle of something."

"Nothing I can't put off," Gina answered. "I need to get some fresh air anyway and could use a break from my homework."

"Thanks, Gina. I put some money on the table in the hall. Make sure you don't forget it."

"Don't worry, Mom. I got it!" she

said as she stuffed the bills into her purse.

The store was just a few blocks away. That was one of the reasons Mom liked where they lived. In case they needed something like milk or cereal, they could easily walk or ride their bikes to the store and didn't need to drive the car.

A few minutes later, Mom heard the front door slam and knew Gina was on her way. *It's really great,* she thought, *to have such a responsible daughter.* Gina had never given her any trouble, was always helpful, and never minded going on errands for her. It was as if Gina knew that being a single mom wasn't always easy. Mom felt blessed, indeed.

When Gina got to the store, she was surprised there were so many people shopping. She picked up the newspaper and got in line behind three others who were waiting to checkout.

What's taking so long? Gina wondered. *I need to get home and finish my homework.* Frustrated and somewhat bored, Gina began to look at all the interesting items right next to her on the shelf: chapstick, little flashlights, batteries, gum, candy bars. *Ummm,* she thought, *Caramel Joy, my favorite.* She picked up the candy bar and looked at it. *No, I don't really need this,* she thought and then started to put it down. *But it would taste so good— and I didn't eat much breakfast.* She had plenty of money to buy the newspaper and the candy bar, but . . . she hesitated. On impulse, she picked up the candy bar and casually dropped it into her purse. She then quickly glanced around to see if anyone had seen her, then turned back to watch the person in front of her as he checked out.

Suddenly, she felt someone tapping her on the shoulder. "Would you step out of line please?" asked an official-looking man whose name tag read, "Ed Perkins, Store Manager."

"What? Me?" she asked, looking somewhat confused. This had never happened to her before.

She followed the man to a small cubicle, which served as an office. He asked her to sit down, and, without saying another word, pushed the play button on the surveillance video.

To Gina's horror, she saw herself standing in the checkout line, casually looking over the items beside her, and then picking up the candy bar and dropping it in her purse. It was the first time she had ever done such a thing—and she had gotten caught!

"Please hand me the candy bar you put into your bag," the manager said. Gina hung her head in shame. She reached into her purse and pulled out the Caramel Joy. She had the money to pay for the candy bar. Her mother wouldn't have cared if she had purchased it. *I've never stolen a thing in my life! What have I done?*

After learning her name, Mr. Perkins said, "Gina, I need to call your mother and explain the procedure we use when someone is caught stealing. I'll need your number, please."

Gina's voice shook as she gave him her mom's telephone number. He picked up his cell phone, excused himself, and when he was out of Gina's hearing, he dialed the number.

Mom was shocked to hear what her daughter had done. Gina had always been so trustworthy. It made her very sad to learn that she had been caught shoplifting. "Oh, Mr. Perkins. I'm so sorry. Gina has never done anything like this before."

"I'm sure that's true," he sympathized. "I've seen her in the store a number of times and she's always been very responsible. But let me explain what we do to teach kids that stealing never pays. If the parents give their permission, we call the police. They will come to the store, handcuff the child, put them in the patrol car, and take them down to the police station where they are questioned by an officer. Then the parents are called to come pick up their child. Usually this experience scares the child so much that the kid never wants to steal again—especially if it's their first offense. What do you want me to do?" Mr. Perkins asked.

Mom swallowed hard. "I think you should do exactly what you've explained. It's a tough lesson for Gina to have to learn, but one of the most important in life. You can have the police call me at this same number."

Meanwhile, Gina waited anxiously for Mr. Perkins to return. She was hoping that her mother would explain that she was a good girl, would never do it again, and insist that she should be released. Gina nearly fell off her chair when the manager came back into his office and said, "I notified your mom that the police are on their way. She will meet you at the station."

"But," Gina tried to defend herself, "I've never stolen anything else in my life. And it was only a candy bar. I have enough money to pay for it. Please take the money. Here it is . . . let me go."

"I'm sorry," the manager said. "If someone commits a crime, they deserve to be punished."

A few minutes later, a patrol car drove up out front. Two policemen walked into the store and back to the manager's office. They handcuffed Gina and escorted her out of the store, through the crowds of people who stood watching, and into the police car. Gina thought she was going to die from embarrassment!

By the time Gina reached the police station, she was in tears. They escorted her into an interrogation room and questioned her. They explained that if Mr. Perkins decided to prosecute her, she would have to appear before a judge who had been known to send kids who have committed crimes to juvenile hall.

Gina trembled as the policeman picked up the phone to call the store manager.

"Hello. Mr. Perkins, what have you decided to do?"

When Gina tearfully promised to never shoplift again, Mr. Perkins said that this one time he would be lenient and allow the police to release Gina into the custody of her mother. Until then, she would have to wait in a jail cell.

It seemed like it took forever for her mom to get there. As Gina sat behind those steel bars, she promised herself and God that she would never, ever, EVER, steal again. ■

Better to have little, with godliness,
than to be rich and dishonest.
—Proverbs 16:8, NLT

Produce Payback

"Carlos, don't kick the ball so hard. If it gets past us, it'll roll all the way to the riverbed."

"I'm just trying to be a good soccer player," Carlos yelled to his brothers. "You just want to win."

"We just don't want to chase the ball down the canyon!"

It was a challenge living on the rocky hillside at the base of the San Bernardino Mountains. Wherever you went, it was either uphill or downhill. Papa was the caretaker of this property and he thought it was the most beautiful land this side of Mexico. It reminded him of where he grew up. But other than the nine acres of apples, which was the land owner's commercial crop, there wasn't much more than sagebrush, weeds, and few tall eucalyptus trees that grew there.

"The city is no place to raise my *niños*," Papa had told his wife. "They need to learn to work, to grow produce, and to make things with their hands."

The boys thought Papa's favorite saying was "idleness is the devil's workshop," because every time they would ask, "Oh, Papa, can't we play?" that's what they would hear.

The family's main job was to irrigate, weed, prune, spray, pick, and finally, haul the apples to market.

But if a thousand apple trees weren't enough to keep the boys busy, Papa soon brought home some more work. "Mama! Carlos! Roberto! Felix! Come! Look what I have for you . . . fruit trees we can plant around the house for our very own use."

Four years later, when the trees were all producing and Mama had her summer garden, the Vasquez family was growing almost all of their own food.

The only disadvantage of living a mile off the main highway and down a bumpy dirt road was that they didn't get many visitors. That's why Mama was so surprised, as she was hanging out the wash, to see a stranger come walking toward her.

"*Hola, cómo está usted?* What can I do for you?" Mama asked.

"I've come to show you some wonderful Christian books."

"*En español?*"

"*Sí,*" the man replied.

Mama called to the boys who were busy weeding, "Look, boys! Come here." Then sitting down at the picnic table, the salesman showed them the most wonderful books they had ever seen. Mama was most interested in the ten beautiful hardcover books that told the story of the history of man from Creation right down to the Bible prophecies about the future.

"*Cuánto cuesta?*" (How much?) she asked.

When she heard the price, she shook her head. "*Muy caro!* Too much! We don't have that much money. And, even if we did, Papa is not a Christian and would not allow us to buy such expensive Christian books. I'm sorry. I really wish I could afford them."

All this time, Carlos was listening carefully. He could see how sad Mama was that she couldn't get the books. She loved to read and sometimes it was lonely for her since she lived too far away for friends to visit. If she had the books to read, she wouldn't be so lonely.

The salesman understood, and then gave Mama a small book that had his name and telephone number printed in it, just in case she changed her mind. Then he packed up the beautiful books and walked back down the dusty road.

Carlos and his mama watched the man until he rounded the bend in the road and was out of sight. "Maybe someday we'll have enough money to buy nice books like that," she sighed.

Carlos didn't say anything, but he was already planning how he could raise the money to buy the books for Mama. The first thing he had to do was check with the friends whose house was at the end of their dirt road next to the highway.

"Mama," he called as he wheeled his bike from the storage shed, "may I ride down to the end of the road and see the Barretts?"

"Sure," said Mom. "Just make sure you're home before dark."

An hour later, Carlos was discussing his plan with his friends. "The roadside fruit stand you have . . . it's on an honor system, right? People just put their money in the slot on the top of the box and then take what they have purchased. Have you ever had trouble with people not paying?"

"Not that we know of. We count how many bags of oranges we leave out there—and usually the money in the metal box is pretty close."

"Good," said Carlos, "because I was wondering if you wanted to sell anything else at your stand."

"We don't have anything else to sell. We only grow oranges."

"Well, we grow lots of things: avocados, lemons, limes, persimmons, apples, and all kinds of vegetables like tomatoes, peppers, and squash. I was wondering if we could put our produce out on your stand."

"Why, I think that's a great idea!" Mrs. Barrett said enthusiastically. "The more people we have stopping for other produce, the more oranges they will buy."

Carlos went on to explain further. He would work hard taking care of his mama's garden and the fruit trees around their house, and when they had extra produce, he would bag and price it and bring it to the Barrett's fruit stand. When the Barretts opened the metal box and counted out their share of the money for the oranges, they could give the rest to him.

"Why are you working so hard on that garden?" his brothers asked. "Why don't you come play soccer with us?"

"I'm trying to earn some extra money," Carlos replied.

"What for?" they asked.

But Carlos would only say, "It's a secret."

One day, close to the end of summer, Carlos stopped by the Barrett's house and asked to count the produce money. He was close to his goal. It wouldn't be much longer and he would be able to order the books. "Good thing we have two apple trees of our own that are loaded," he commented to the Barretts, "because it's pretty much the end of our garden produce."

The apples sold well. Four weeks later, Carlos had the money and called the phone number that was written in the little book the salesman had given them.

When the man came trudging back up the dusty road, Mama ran out and explained that she still couldn't afford the books.

"Don't worry," the salesman said. "Carlos ordered these—and he says he has the money."

"What?" exclaimed Mama. "He does?" Then it suddenly occured to her why he had been working so hard all summer. "And here I thought he was just trying to stay out of the devil's workshop!"

"Happy Mother's Day! Sorry, it's a little late," Carlos said all out of breath from running down the road to catch up with her. "Or maybe it's an early Christmas present. Anyway, Mama, I just wanted you to have the books. It was worth all the hard work just to see you this happy! Besides, work isn't *really work* when you're doing it for someone you *really love*."

Mama was so shocked she didn't know who or what to hug first . . . the book salesman, the books she wanted so badly, or Carlos. In the end, she hugged all three, but Carlos got the biggest hug of all. ■

And let our people also learn to maintain good works, to meet urgent needs, that they may not be unfruitful.
—Titus 3:14, NKJV

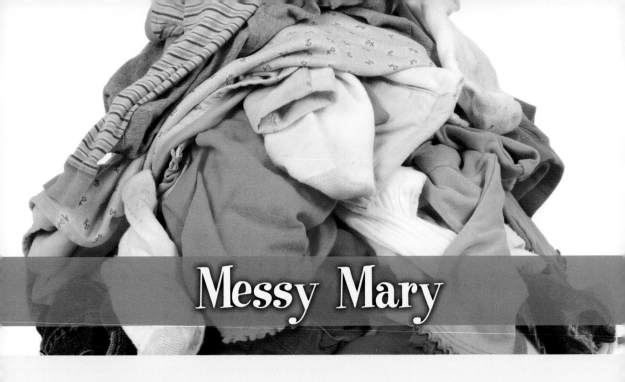

Messy Mary

“**C**ome on, Mary. We're going to be late! It's past time to go.”

“I know, Mom, but I can't find my sandals,” Mary shouted down the hall.

“When did you have them last?” Mom questioned, trying to be helpful.

“Yesterday. I think I wore them when I went to the pool with the Martins.”

“Did you have them on when you came home?”

“I think so.”

“Then they've got to be around the house somewhere.”

“Oh forget it! I'll just wear my sneakers,” Mary said. She was frustrated and angry with herself.

On the way to get groceries, Mom spoke up. “You know, Mary, if you would put your clothes in your hamper when they need washing, and if you would put your shoes on the shoe rack in your closet, you would save yourself a whole lot of time looking for things." Mary sensed the lecture was just beginning.

"Since it's spring break, I want you to take out everything that's thrown in your closet or under your bed and organize your things."

"Oh, Mom," Mary replied. "My room isn't that bad! Besides, it's *my* room, why can't I keep it the way I want?"

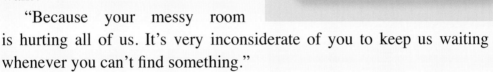

"Because your messy room is hurting all of us. It's very inconsiderate of you to keep us waiting whenever you can't find something."

"Yeah, I know," said Mary in a disgruntled manner.

"I want you to start on this project as soon as we get home."

"Yes, ma'am," Mary responded. She didn't like it when Mom got on her case, but Mary knew she was right. And she knew her mom wasn't the only one who had noticed how she kept her room. Her dad didn't call her his little *Messy Mary* for nothing!

Back home, Mary went straight to her room and closed the door. She looked around.

Where should I begin? She spotted her library book sticking out from under a pile of papers on her desk. She remembered she was in the middle of reading an exciting chapter. *I should read that first, then get to the pile of stuff on the floor and the clothes hanging out of the opened dresser drawers.*

As Mom finished putting the groceries away, she thought it was rather quiet in Mary's room, so she peeked in to see how Mary was doing with her re-organization project. Mary heard her coming and quickly jumped up. "I was just taking a break, Mom. I'll get back to cleaning in a few minutes," she called.

"Have you found your sandals yet?"

"No, not yet, but I will eventually," Mary replied.

The next morning, everyone was getting ready for church. "Are you ready, Mary?" Mom called down the hall.

"One minute, Mom!" Mary responded with panic in her voice. She couldn't find her church dress. Finally, in desperation, she looked under her bed. After pulling out two notebooks, a purse, three shoes, a pair of jeans, and two tops, she spotted her dress. She pulled out a rumpled up mess, with a stain on the front from the spaghetti she spilled on herself at last week's fellowship dinner.

"Oh, no!" she panicked. "What should I wear?"

On a hanger in the closet was an old skirt. She put it on. "I guess I'll have to wear it even if it's a little tight." She also found an un-ironed blouse that sort of matched, so she put it on.

Mary dashed out of her bedroom and down the hall to the car where everyone was waiting. She slumped down in the backseat. No one made a comment about what she was wearing. At church, she was horrified because her outfit was so unlike the pretty dress she usually wore. She hoped that no one would notice.

After lunch, the family was invited to her friend Taylor's house, so Mary found herself in that snug outfit for the whole afternoon. No one said a word about her clothes, but Mary had never felt so humiliated. She determined it would never happen again. She had to clean her room.

That evening, the phone rang. It was Josie. "Mary, are you coming?"

"What do you mean?"

"Have you forgotten? Ben's birthday party is tonight. We're waiting for you down at the skating rink. Just don't forget to bring the special invitation Ben gave you. It's your ticket to get in."

Mary had completely forgotten about the party. The kids in her class

Photo taken by: cqgraphicdesign.com

looked forward to Ben's birthday parties each year because his mom and dad always planned some special activity and served delicious food. "Mom! Mom!" Mary went rushing into the kitchen, "Mom, I forgot that tonight is Ben's birthday party at the skating rink. Can I go?"

"Sure, honey. We'll leave as soon as you're ready."

Mary went back to her room to find the invitation. Where had she put it? Ben had given it to her right before break. She had brought it home. *It must be on my desk,* she thought. *What a mess,* she said to herself as she began sorting through the piles of papers, books, trash, and left-over items from her school lunches. She had to find that invitation or she couldn't get into the rink.

"Are you ready?" Mom called from the bottom of the stairs. "I'll pick up a few things for breakfast while I'm out."

Where is that invitation? Maybe it was in her coat pocket or stuck in her dirty lunch box that she had dumped on the floor of her room rather than unpacking it in the kitchen and washing it out. Why hadn't she put the invitation on her bulletin board so she would know where it was? The words of her dad rang in her ears, *"Mary, I made you a bulletin board where you can post important notices and papers, so you will always know where they are."*

She was so frustrated with herself, she began to cry. *Why, oh why, didn't I put that invitation on my bulletin board?*

A few minutes later, Mom came into her room. "Aren't you going to the party?"

"I guess not," moaned Mary. "I can't find my invitation and they won't let me in without it."

"I'm sorry," Mom sympathized. "I'm sure you're disappointed. I know Ben's parties are the highlight of the year, and you've been looking forward to it for months."

After searching for thirty minutes and still not finding the invitation, Mary threw up her hands and shook her head. "I give up!"

Realizing that she couldn't go the party, Mary threw herself down on the bed and cried. After a few minutes, she sat up and looked around. "What a mess! I am going to clean this room if it takes me all night!" she decided.

Before she went to bed, the room was spotless, without a thing out of place. Even her bulletin board was organized.

She even found the missing invitation. It was stuck between the pages of her math book—too bad she found it too late. And her sandals?

They showed up under a pile of clothes.

Mary took one more look around to make sure everything was in place and then called for her mom and dad to inspect her work.

"Wow," said Mom, "I can't believe your room is so clean. I'm really proud of you."

"Me too," said Dad. "And to help you remember to keep it this way, I printed you something special for your bulletin board."

Mary reached out and took the paper, reading out loud, " 'Let all things be done decently and in order,' 1 Corinthians 14:40."

"Thank you, Dad," Mary exclaimed as she ran over and gave him a great big hug. "With this reminder and with Jesus' help—I'll try really hard not to be *Messy Mary* again." ∎

Let all things be done decently and in order.
—1 Corinthians 14:40, NKJV

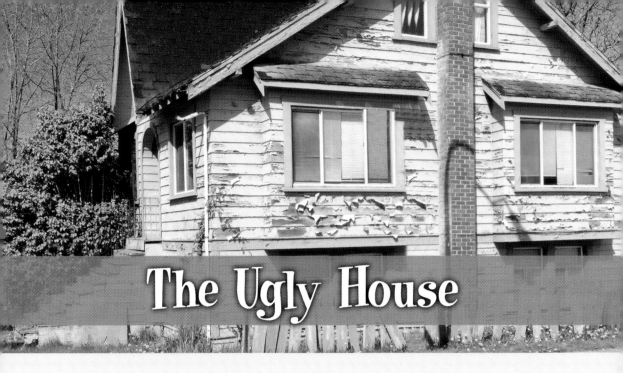

The Ugly House

Carter stood on the playground, his face pressed against the chain-link fence. He stared at the house across the street—the house that all the kids made fun of. They called it all kinds of names, but Carter called it just one name—*home*.

The bell rang and everyone started toward the door of the school, lining up according to their classrooms. Carter joined the rest of Miss Butler's class, listening as the kids chattered like monkeys. Carter just stared at the ground.

It had been three months since his father had moved him and his brother, Jeff, into the house across from the school. Before the move, they had all been excited. Dad had hoped that the new job would work out and that he and the boys would finally have enough to eat. They had packed up their truck and made the long drive, only to find out the job wasn't there anymore. The only place they could afford was the broken-

down house across from the school.

Carter knew his dad worked hard. He spent long hours every day looking for work, and the rest of the time he spent fixing things up around the house, trying to make it look better. He worked in their garden, growing fresh vegetables and then prepared delicious meals. He always offered to help Carter and Jeff with homework and took time to play games in the evening. His dad really was the best dad in the whole world!

Carter listened as the kids in line talked about what they were doing after school. Just once, Carter wished he had a friend to go home with. He would love to go somewhere else besides the broken-down house across the street.

The students filed into the classroom and sat at their desks, waiting for Miss Butler's announcement. "OK everyone, settle down now. I'm going to assign partners for the science project. The assignments will be done randomly . . . here goes."

Carter listened as names were called and happy chatter filled the room.

"Mick, you'll be working with Carter." Snickers accompanied the announcement and Carter looked at Mick. He definitely didn't look happy, but he didn't protest either. The students moved around to find quiet spots to discuss their projects.

"Want to come over to my house tonight . . . to work?" Mick hesitated. "I guess you can probably stay for dinner if you want."

"I can ask my dad." Carter didn't look up as he answered.

"You know where I live? It's the brick house next to the firestation." Mick looked around, embarrassed.

Carter nodded and shuffled the papers around on his desk. The bell rang and everyone hurried out the door. Carter tagged along behind the others as usual. He always dragged his feet, hoping they wouldn't see him crossing the street to his home.

"Dad?" Carter called.

"In here, buddy." Carter followed his dad's voice to the kitchen where he was chopping up vegetables from their garden. "How was school?" He stopped working and put his hand on Carter's shoulder.

"OK," Carter squirmed. "We were assigned partners for the science project. Mick asked if I could come to his house to work tonight and maybe stay for dinner."

"Would you like that?" Carter's dad looked into his eyes.

"I guess."

"Well then, Jeff and I will miss you. Have fun. If you need any help, you know all you have to do is ask."

"Well, actually, we're supposed to come up with a science project. Do you have any ideas?"

"*Hmmm* . . . let me think. How about . . ." Dad proceeded to tell him all about an experiment to make a battery.

When he finished, Carter's face beamed. "Thanks Dad, you're the greatest!"

A few minutes later, Carter knocked on Mick's front door.

"Yes?" Mick's mom answered the door, looking like she was in a hurry.

"I'm here to work with . . ."

The woman turned and let the door slam, cutting Carter off. "Mick!"

"Oh . . . ah . . . um . . . hi, Carter. Come in." Mick said hesitantly as he held the door open. Carter looked around, surprised. He had expected to find that Mick's house was special. From the outside, it looked so nice. But inside, there was clutter everywhere.

"See you later. Grab supper from the freezer." Mick's mom let the door slam behind her. Mick frowned.

"I guess we can work over here." Mick pushed a bunch of papers to the end of the dining table, clearing some room. "Do you have any ideas about what we can do?"

"Well," Carter hesitated, "my dad had an idea. What if we did something with batteries? We can show how they work, make one on our own, and start something with it."

"Yeah, that's a cool idea." Mick actually smiled a little.

"My dad's good at that kind of stuff. He said he'd help us . . . if we want him to."

"He would, really?" Mick seemed surprised. "My parents don't have time to help me. Mom's always off to some meeting and Dad's always working." Mick looked sad. "Do you really think your dad would help us get started?"

"Sure, he's always willing to help me."

"Can we ask him now?" Mick looked hopeful.

"Sure, but . . ." Carter hesitated, "but, you'd have to come to my house." Carter was so embarrassed. He knew Mick wouldn't want to step foot in his home.

"Well, OK. I guess we can do that."

Carter looked at Mick, surprised. "Um, I guess we could go down there now . . . if your parents don't mind."

Mick looked even sadder. "They don't care as long as I'm home before dark."

Mick looked at the broken-down home where Carter lived. On the outside, it really was a little ugly. He followed Carter into the house and was surprised. Everything was neat and clean, and he smelled something wonderful cooking on the stove.

"Dad?" Carter called.

"In here." He appeared at the kitchen door, a loaf of homemade bread in his hand. "Oh, you're back. This must be Mick. Glad to meet you," he reached out to shake Mick's hand. "Will you be staying for dinner?" he smiled.

"I guess I can . . . Mom didn't have anything ready." Mick was really surprised. This wasn't what he expected at all.

Dinner was delicious. It had been a long time since Mick had enjoyed a homemade meal. Carter and Jeff laughed and joked around with him so much that he couldn't remember the last time he had so much fun! And he loved the stories that Carter's dad told.

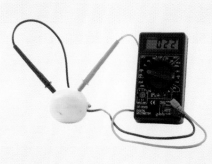

After dinner, they all cleaned up the kitchen together and then Carter's dad helped them get started on their science project. Before Mick knew it, it was time to go home.

"I think you boys will do just great." Carter's dad patted them both on their shoulders.

"Can we work again tomorrow?" Mick seemed excited. "I think our project can win the science fair."

"Sure!" Carter exclaimed. It had been fun working with Mick. "I'll meet you at your house after school?"

Mick hesitated. He didn't want anyone to know that he had been inside Carter's broken-down house. But, the house wasn't anything like he expected, and Carter's dad and brother were great. To be honest, he hadn't thought about the outside of the house all evening. He was too busy having a good time.

"How about . . . we come here?" Mick suggested. "This was kind of fun. Your dad's the best."

"Really?" Carter was surprised.

"Yeah, I'll be over right after school. I can't wait to work on this project some more."

Carter looked around at his house. Maybe it was ugly on the outside, but inside it was filled with love. They didn't have much, but what they did have, they were willing to share.

"Sure, sounds good!"

"Great. I better get home." Mick grabbed his things and headed for the door. "Thanks, Carter. I had a great time." He walked away, no longer embarrassed to be seen at the ugly house. ■

> "The LORD does not look at the things man looks at.
> Man looks at the outward appearance,
> but the LORD looks at the heart."
> —1 Samuel 16:7, NIV

Blasting the Bullies

It was a long bus ride, especially when you didn't have any friends. Justin tried to review the words for his spelling test. He had practiced them last night until he was pretty sure he could get them all correct. But the noise in the seats up front was so distracting. They were at it again—the bullies. This morning they were taunting Lolita about her hair. It was braided along the sides of her head and two more long braids hung down her back. None of the other girls wore their hair that way. So that made her hairstyle more noticeable.

He was new to this school and he really didn't like riding the school bus all that much. It wasn't the ride. It was the noise, both from the other kids and the music the bus driver chose to blare over the speakers—probably to drown out the kids. For Justin, the morning hours were for last minute studying, planning his day, and praying. All of which was difficult on the noisy bus.

Justin had noticed Lolita the very

first day he got on the bus. She sat alone near the front with her face pushed against the window, just staring at the roadside as it went by. Justin chose a seat one row back and to the right. His was one of the first stops, so there weren't many kids on board yet; just he and Lolita and an older student who sat in the very back.

It didn't take long for the bus to fill up. Justin noticed several boys sat in the seats surrounding Lolita. It looked to him like they had chosen those seats on purpose. He soon found out his suspicions were right.

"Where did you shop this year, Lolita? Goodwill or the Salvation Army?" Derek shoved his knee into the back of Lolita's seat, pushing her forward.

"I think it was someone's yard sale. Stinkin' pink is so your color," Aaron added.

The whole group laughed loudly. Justin's stomach did a funny belly flop. He noticed the bus driver looked back in his mirror, but he didn't say anything or let on that he had heard.

Every morning for the last three months, it was the same. The group surrounded Lolita and aimed their carefully crafted jabs her way. To them, it was entertainment. To

Justin, it was sickening. But who was he to stand up to the group of bullies? Justin prayed every day that God would show him how to help Lolita.

One spring morning, as Justin waited for the bus, he had an idea. *Why don't I sit in the seat behind Lolita? At least, I could protect her from Derek and Aaron.* He wasn't sure how they would react to finding him in their usual seat, but it was worth a try.

Lolita watched Justin get on the bus and seemed surprised when he sat behind her. He wasn't sure, but when she turned her face back toward the window, he thought he saw a faint smile. Justin waited for two more stops, and then Derek and Aaron pushed each other on to the bus and down the aisle, stopping at their usual place.

"What's up, bro?" Derek challenged Justin.

Justin just shrugged his shoulders and didn't look up. They plopped

down in the seat across the aisle. Soon the bus was full, and Derek and Aaron started chatting with their group about a basketball game they had watched. They forgot all about picking on Lolita until they got off the bus. Then, all the way to her classroom, they teased her about her tattered backpack.

Lolita turned around once and looked Justin's way. He was sure now that what he saw was indeed a smile.

After school, Justin hurried to the bus stop. He made sure he got on before Derek and Aaron and their gang. Again, he plopped down behind Lolita. When she turned his way, he smiled, and said a quick, "Hello."

The gang wasn't happy about Justin's choice. They made it clear with the dirty looks they gave him. But they were shorter than Justin, who was tall for his age. At least he had that going for him, along with all of his prayers. Maybe God was leading him to help in some way.

One day, Justin was surprised when Derek and Aaron sat in front of Lolita while the rest of the gang sat in the seats surrounding them. He had a feeling that something was up. When the door shut, Aaron grabbed an apple from  his backpack and started throwing it around the bus over Lolita's head, coming close to hitting her several times.

"Hey, what do girls like you do on their vacations? I bet no one invites you over," Derek turned and poked his face close to Lolita.

"Going to visit the thrift store?" Aaron added his jab.

Comments were soon flying all around him, barbs that Justin knew must hurt Lolita. He quietly started to pray. And that's when he did what he never thought he would have the courage to do.

Justin stood up and towered over the bullies. "Leave her alone," he said in a forceful voice. "Just . . . leave . . . her . . . alone!"

The bus suddenly got deathly silent. It felt like the quiet before a storm and Justin expected that storm to strike at any minute.

But it never came.

Derek and Aaron looked at Justin in shock. They didn't know what to say, so they didn't say anything at all—not to Lolita or anyone else.

When the bus came to Justin's stop, he gathered up his things and stood up to leave.

All of sudden, he heard a soft voice that very faintly said, "Thank you."

Justin turned back and saw something he knew he would remember the rest of his life. Lolita's face was lit up by a smile that stretched from ear to ear.

Justin nodded and smiled back.

He knew his courage had come from the One who had faced bullies Himself. It made Justin feel good to realize that he had followed Jesus' example by helping those who weren't able to stand up for themselves. ■

Deliver the poor and needy;
free them from the hand of the wicked.
—Psalm 82:4, NKJV

The Brave "Chicken"

Mark flopped backward on to the grass, his chest heaving from running so hard. "That's it," he said. "I'm done." He had been playing soccer with Jack, Mitchell, Juan, and Lamar for over an hour in Jack's backyard, like they did most afternoons, and the competition had been fierce.

Mitchell slumped beside him, the soccer ball in his arms. "Me too. Who won?"

"I don't know," said Jack, stealing the ball from Mitchell as he ran past, "but last one inside is a rotten egg."

Mitchell jumped to his feet and was after Jack in an instant, with Juan and Lamar following close behind. Mark laughed as his friends pushed and shoved their way through the back door, jostling to be first, and he wandered inside to join them.

By the time Mark arrived in the kitchen, everyone's glass was empty and there was only one cookie left

on the plate. Mark raised an eyebrow in surprise.

Jack grinned at him. "You snooze, you lose," he said and handed Mark a glass of milk. "And hurry up. There's something I want to show you guys. Mom will be home soon so we've got to be quick."

Mark gulped down the milk and grabbed the cookie from the counter before taking the stairs two at a time to join the others in Jack's room.

Jack and Lamar were sitting on the bed while Mitchell and Juan were sitting on the floor, their backs leaning against the wall. Mark sat down beside them just as Jack reached under his bed and pulled out a bottle of beer.

"No way, man," said Juan. "Where did you get that?"

"From my older brother, Tony," said Jack. "He got it from one of his friends at school who stole it from his dad's fridge."

"Cool," said Lamar. "Have you tried it yet?"

Jack shook his head. "Nah, I figured I'd share it with you guys." He twisted the lid off and air bubbles escaped from the bottle of beer with a hiss.

"Your mom will kill you if she finds out," said Mitchell.

"She won't though, will she?" said Jack.

"You hope," said Mitchell.

Jack ignored him. "So, who wants some?"

Mark watched as, one by one, his friends tasted alcohol for the first time.

Lamar took a sip, screwed up his face, and said, "That's disgusting."

Juan ran to the bathroom and spat his down the sink. He came back into the room and shuddered. "People actually pay to drink that stuff? It's revolting."

Jack put the bottle to his lips and took a swig. Mark could see him struggling to swallow, but Jack pretended to like it. "Not bad," he said. "I could get used to that." He then burped loudly and jumped off his bed, staggering around the room like he was drunk, much to the amusement of Juan and Lamar. Mark just thought he looked stupid. Mitchell wasn't saying anything at all.

Jack lurched towards Mark and held the bottle out towards him. "What about you? Are you in or out?"

Mark's heart beat fast in his chest, and he hesitated for just a moment. Of course, he liked hanging around with his friends and he was always up for a bit of fun, but this was different. He said a silent prayer and knew what he should do. "Thanks, Jack, but I'm going to pass."

Jack leaned down close to Mark's face, his beer-breath making Mark cringe. "What? Are you chicken or something?" Lamar and Juan laughed and started making clucking noises.

"Nope. I just don't want to," said Mark, giving Jack a shove back on to his bed.

"He's scared his mom will find out," said Lamar.

"Poor baby," said Jack. "He's scared of his mommy." Jack pretended to cry like a baby.

"Or maybe he doesn't think he's man enough to handle it," Juan teased.

"My uncle says it puts hair on your chest," said Lamar.

"I'm actually rather attached to my brain cells," Mark replied. "You can kill yours off with that stuff if you like, but I'm not going to join you."

"Come on, Mark, have some," said Jack. "It's only beer. It's not like it's going to kill you or anything."

Mark stood up and looked around at his friends. "I'm out of here," he announced. "Anyone want to come to the skate park with me? We could fit in a few runs on the half-pipe before it gets dark."

Mitchell scurried to Mark's side, looking relieved. "I'll come."

"Great," said Mark, thumping Mitchell on the arm. "Let's go. Catch you guys tomorrow."

Mark could hear Jack, Juan, and Lamar making chicken noises as he left. *Cluck, cluck, cluck.* Then they called out, "Mark's a chicken! Mark's a chicken," but he kept on walking without saying a word. Mitchell followed a few steps behind.

Mark and Mitchell rode their skate-boards in silence along the sidewalk for a while until Mitchell finally spoke. "Thanks for that. I didn't really want to drink alcohol, but I wasn't sure how I was going to get out of it."

"Don't let them push you around," said Mark. "If you don't want to, just tell them No. They'll give you a hard time, but they'll get over it."

"If my mom or dad smelled beer on me when I got home, I'd be grounded for life. I just couldn't take the risk," said Mitchell. "Is that why you didn't try it too?"

"Partly," said Mark. He took a moment to think about how he was going to explain it to Mitchell. "Sure, my mom and dad would be mad if they found out I'd been drinking, but it's more than that. Alcohol isn't good for your body and I want to make the soccer team this year, so I need to keep myself as fit as possible. I also don't like the fact that people do foolish things when they're drunk. They lose control and do stuff they normally wouldn't do and then have to live with the consequences the next day." Mark jumped his skateboard over a bump in the sidewalk. "But that's not the real reason. You know that sermon Pastor Rick preached last week?"

"Kind of," said Mitchell. "I listened to some of it."

"He was talking about how we need to keep a relationship with Jesus at the top of our priority list. There are things that help us have a strong relationship, such as reading our Bibles and praying and doing things to help other people; and there are things that get in the way of that relationship."

Mark shrugged. "I guess I just think that drinking is something that would get in the way of my relationship with Jesus. If I can't think straight, how will I know if Jesus is trying to teach me something?"

"That's a pretty good reason," said Mitchell. "It makes a lot of sense when you put it like that."

"Nah, it's not just a *good reason*," said Mark. "It's the *best*. Come on, I'll race you to the half-pipe." ∎

"If you belonged to the world, it would love you. . . . You do not belong to the world, but I have chosen you out of the world. That is why the world hates you."
—John 15:19, NIV

Patty's Patch

"Just two more weeks until summer camp! I can hardly wait!" Patty exclaimed to her mom as she marked a big red *X* on the calendar. "I want to start packing. I don't want to forget anything. Do you know where my suitcase is?"

"In the hall closet," Mom replied.

Patty retrieved her bright red suitcase and started going down the list of items the campers were to bring—a warm jacket for sitting around the campfire, heavy socks for hiking, a bathing suit, a toothbrush, a flashlight, a Bible . . . the list went on and on.

"Seven more days," she announced to her parents at breakfast a week later. "By this time next Sunday, we'll be half-way to Sunshine Meadows Adventure Camp!"

The night before they were to leave, Patty was so excited that she could hardly go to sleep. She was thinking about all the fun activity classes at camp. She especially loved the patches

she received from completing the class requirements. Last year, she had gotten patches for horseback riding, hiking, and swimming. Every summer she added new patches to the sash she wore over her girls' club uniform.

Patty didn't know what classes she would take this year, but she was hoping for the wildflower patch and the one for astronomy. The camp had a new telescope and looking at the moon, planets, and stars would be fun.

But the patch Patty had her heart set on receiving the most was the coveted Honor Camper patch. It was the top award given to only one camper per day based upon being kind, courteous, and helpful. To receive this patch, a camper needed to be nominated by a staff member. Patty wanted to win that nomination more than anything!

The Honor Camper patch was a very special award indeed! Every night all the campers would meet for worship in the woods. They enjoyed singing wonderful songs about Jesus. Songs such as "He's Able," "Peace Like a River," and "Kum Ba Yah." One of the staff would share a Bible story—and there was always a special skit.

Patty loved campfires. There was something special about sitting next to a good friend, watching and smelling a crackling fire, singing songs, and listening to stories out under the stars.

But for Patty, the very best part came at the end of the program. After closing prayer, the camp director would announce who had won the Honor Camper patch for that day. She was saving a special place on her sash for that patch!

Morning finally came, and it was time to leave for camp. After Dad put her suitcase and camping gear into the trunk of the car, Mom and Patty were ready for their three-hour trip.

As they were driving away, Dad called out, "Hope your dream comes true about the Honor Camper patch!"

During the very first campfire of the week, the director explained how an honor camper was chosen. The counselors and staff would be on the lookout for campers who were kind, courteous, helpful, and obedient regardless of the circumstances. They would then have a meeting and choose the honor camper from the names nominated. At the end of the campfire worship, the award would be presented.

Every night at campfire, when the director was about to make the announcement, Patty would hold her breath, close her eyes, and pray that her name would be called!

Monday night, Tina, the girl who had gone out of her way to make friends with a homesick camper was picked. *Maybe Tuesday, it will be me,* Patty thought hopefully.

But Tuesday, Missy, the most cheerful girl in camp was chosen. Everyone noticed that whenever anything went wrong, Missy always came up with a positive comment.

Maybe Wednesday I'll get the Honor Camper patch, Patty thought. *Tomorrow I'll look for extra ways to be courteous and helpful. Surely someone will notice me!*

But Wednesday night, Diane was chosen for her willingness to pray with her friends and share Jesus.

Maybe Thursday! Patty was going to make certain that her counselor, Miss Nancy, noticed how helpful she was.

Each day, the campers were assigned chores. On Thursday, Patty's unit was assigned kitchen duty. They were responsible for washing dishes, sweeping and mopping the floor, and emptying the trash. Another unit was assigned to the dining room. They were to clean the floor and wipe down the tables.

Miss Nancy was very young and pretty and all the girls loved her. The other counselor, Mrs. Wilson, had worked at camp for years and pretty much ran the place! Patty had known her all of her life. Even though Patty loved her, sometimes Mrs. Wilson could be very bossy!

Patty and her unit were busy in the kitchen cleaning when Mrs. Wilson came in and interrupted their work. "I need some extra workers out in the dining room. It's a mess out there! You have more than enough help in the kitchen. I need three of you to come with me. Hurry up! I haven't got all day!" she ordered.

Even though Miss Nancy was in charge of Patty's unit, her counselor was not about to cross Mrs. Wilson. So she picked Patty and a couple of the other girls to go clean the dining room.

Patty had barely finished cleaning the tables, when Mrs. Wilson ordered her to go back into the kitchen, along with several others. Mrs. Wilson followed them and continued telling them what to do. Then she ordered them back to the dining room. Back and forth, back and forth! *How are we ever going to get done if this keeps up?* Patty wondered. Everyone was getting very frustrated with Mrs. Wilson, but not wanting to make matters worse, Miss Nancy didn't say a word.

Finally, it was more than Patty could stand. Without thinking, the words just tumbled out. "Mrs. Wilson, how in the world are we supposed to get our work done when you keep moving us all around? Why, you aren't even our boss! Miss Nancy is our counselor and she's the one that's supposed to tell us what to do, not you!" Patty said emphatically.

This was exactly what most of the girls were thinking, but dared not say. A hush fell over the room.

Suddenly, Patty realized what she had done. Horrified, she put her hand over her mouth—but it was too late. Like feathers in the wind, she could never take back those horrible words!

Patty quickly ran and threw her arms around Mrs. Wilson. "I'm so sorry! Please forgive me. I should never have said that! I didn't mean to be disrespectful! Really, I didn't!"

Mrs. Wilson gently hugged Patty and said, "Of course, I forgive you. I'm sorry too. I shouldn't have taken over like that. You're right, Miss Nancy is in charge of you and your unit and it wasn't my place to boss you around. But I am very disappointed in the way you responded. I wish you had told me in a respectful way. I'm especially sorry this happened, because I had planned to nominate you tonight for the Honor Camper patch. But after your outburst today, I won't be able to do so! I'm sure you understand."

Patty began to cry. Hearing Mrs. Wilson's words was devastating! What a bitter pill to swallow. If only she could go back and do it over. But it was too late!

Patty didn't receive the Honor Camper patch to sew on her sash. Instead, she earned a far more important award—a patch for her heart for learning the valuable lesson of using self-control and being respectful in every situation. Patty vowed that next year she would be an Honor Camper . . . with or without the patch! ■

> *"Men will have to give account on the day of judgment for every careless word they have spoken."*
> —Matthew 12:36, NIV

Spooky Finds a Home

More than anything else in the world, Brett wanted a pet of his very own. His brother and sister each had one. But according to Dad and Mom, one cat and one dog was quite enough for any normal family.

"But Purrdy is Bryan's cat," Brett complained. "Purrdy even sleeps on Bryan's bed. I want a pet that belongs to me and can sleep on my bed."

"Well," Mom suggested, "what about Spangles?" Spangles was an adorable, floppy-eared, pedigreed Cocker Spaniel. They had gotten her a year ago on the July 4 and named her Spangles in honor of the national anthem, "The Star-Spangled Banner."

"Everyone knows Spangles is Brittany's dog," argued Brett. "Brittany picked her out and she was the one who wanted a female so she could have puppies."

"I'm sure Brittany will share Spangles," Mom said. "You can help feed her."

"Awww, Mom," Brett sighed, "sharing Spangles is not the same as having my very own pet."

But no matter how often Brett brought up the topic of getting a pet, there was always some reason why it wasn't the right time. Sometimes it seemed like their family was too busy to care for another pet.

Months went by. Then one day at church, the pastor announced, "Boys and girls, today we have a special guest who is going to tell you a story. So please come up front and sit quietly." Brett sat down with the rest of the kids and watched as the storyteller opened a small box and lifted out a scrawny, black and white kitten.

"A few nights ago," the lady began, "I was trying to go to sleep when I heard a cat meowing outside our bedroom window. It wasn't just a meow every once in a while — like when a cat wants to come inside — it was a constant high-pitched *meow, meow* like the cat was scared. I wondered why the cat was making all that racket. I tried to cover my head with the pillow so I could go to sleep, but the cat just kept meowing. So, I got up and shut the window. But I could still hear the cat. Finally, I decided that if I was going to be able to sleep, I would have to find the cat and put it someplace where it would stop meowing.

"I got dressed and went outside to see if I could find the cat. I took a flashlight and looked under the bushes in the backyard. No cat. I looked in the shed. No cat. Then I looked up. And way up high above my head, I spotted a tiny little kitten perched on the branch of a tree. I called to the cat, 'Here kitty, kitty,' but it wouldn't come down. I had a feeling the kitten had gotten scared by a dog, climbed the tree, and then didn't know how to turn around on the branch and climb back down. So, I got a ladder and climbed up, reached as high as I could, and lifted the tiny kitten down. The next morning, I asked all the neighbors if they had lost a little kitten, but no one claimed him. So, I decided to bring the kitten to church and see if there would be anyone here who would like to have a lost kitten for their very own. He's still a little scared of people and spooks easily. But with a lot of love, I have a feeling this kitten will make someone a very special pet."

Brett's hand shot up. "I want it! Please, can I have him?"

"Well," the lady said, "ask your parents. If they say Yes, he's yours."

Brett ran back to the pew where his parents were sitting. "Can I have the kitten? Please, Mom! Please, Dad! My birthday's next week—and I've been praying for a pet. Please, can I have it?"

After church, Mom and Dad had a little talk and decided that Brett could have the kitten for his birthday. So that's how Spooky became part of the family and grew up to be a gentle, loving cat who slept at the foot of Brett's bed.

One night a couple of years later, as the family was eating supper, Dad announced, "Kids, something's come up that Mom and I need to talk with you about. As soon as you finish cleaning the kitchen and feeding the animals, let's meet in the family room."

"What's going on?" Brett asked as soon as his older brother and sister were busy washing the dishes and he was alone with Dad.

"Aren't you the curious one?" Dad laughed. "You'll find out soon enough. Why don't you get the animals fed while you're waiting for Brittany and Bryan to finish the dishes?"

Brett shrugged his shoulders and poured a scoopful of dog food into Spangles' bowl and then turned to the two cats who were rubbing up against his legs. He reached down, gave each a pat, and then filled their bowls too.

A few minutes later, the whole family gathered in the family room and listened as Dad explained how he had gotten a call from the Far Eastern Division mission. They needed a principal and a teacher for their mission school in Singapore and had asked if he and Mom and the family would be willing to leave their home in Tulsa, Oklahoma, and be missionaries in Singapore.

"Singapore?" questioned Bryan. "That's halfway around the world."

"It sounds fun," Brittany chimed in. She was always the adventurous one. "We'd get to see lots of different countries."

"But what about our pets?" Brett asked. "Can I take Spooky along?"

"No," Mom explained. "We'd have to find good homes for them here."

And so the decision was made for the family to accept the challenge of mission service in far-off Singapore, while Bryan, Brittany, and Brett started looking for homes for their pets.

Bryan's good friend, Keena, immediately wanted Purrdy. She had visited Bryan's house many times and had already fallen in love with him. It was all planned that she would pick him up the day before the family was to leave for Singapore.

Spangles was a valuable dog. When word got around that Brittany was looking for a good home for her, a number of families said they would love to have Spangles. Brittany finally decided that she would give Spangles to her friends, Lynn and Rylie.

But none of their friends wanted Spooky. Spooky may not have been the prettiest cat—or the most valuable—but to Brett, he was the best, most fun-loving, and playful cat in the whole world! Spooky would make someone a wonderful pet. So, without telling anyone in the family, he began knocking on doors in his neighborhood.

"Hi, I'm Brett, and I live around the corner. My family is going to Singapore as missionaries and we can't take my special cat, Spooky. I'm looking for just the right family who will give the most wonderful cat in the whole world a good home."

"No, I'm sorry," the lady in the two-story stucco house said. "We already have a cat."

"I'm allergic to cats," the man who lived four doors away explained, "otherwise, I'd help you out."

No matter how many excuses Brett heard, he didn't get discouraged. He prayed and continued knocking on doors. "God knows how special Spooky is," he told everyone he met, "so He's not going to let him go to just any home. It has to be the best home in Tulsa."

A couple of blocks away, a kind older man answered the door and said, "I'd love to give Spooky a home. It's very lonely here since my grandkids moved away. And a good cat would keep me company."

Brett was excited and ran all the way home. "Mom, I found a home for Spooky, and I'm going to take him to his new home right away!"

"But we're not leaving for three weeks. Are you sure you don't want to keep him until the last day?"

Tears came to Brett's eyes. "I'd like to keep him as long as possible, but what if he doesn't understand when I leave him at his new home and he tries to find me? If I wait until the last moment, no one would be here to take him back to his new house. I better take him now, just in case."

Every day for the next three weeks, Brett walked by Spooky's new home. Once, he saw Spooky sitting in the window, but he didn't stop. When he really missed Spooky, he imagined him sitting on the old man's lap, being petted, or sleeping in a basket at the foot of the old man's bed. He would miss Spooky— but he smiled, knowing that God had provided just the right home for the best cat in the whole world. ■

And we know that all things work together for good to those who love God.
—Romans 8:28, NKJV

Daredevil Dana

Dana liked to live dangerously. She loved to run, jump, climb, dive, and basically do anything that looked difficult. She wasn't afraid to take chances.

From the time she was a little girl, her parents' warnings were constantly ringing in her ears. *"Be careful!" "Don't get hurt!" "Slow down!" "Don't climb so high!" "Watch where you're going!"* Dana was obedient, so their warnings helped . . . for a little while. However, sometimes she forgot what they said, and she would be off exploring some other risky place or attempting a challenging feat.

One of Dana's favorite activities was climbing trees. She especially liked the tallest ones.

When Dana wasn't climbing trees, she was climbing rocks. She loved going to the mountain lake with her grandpa and grandma where there were huge rocks along the shore. She made a game of jumping from rock to rock.

When it came to sports, Dana was naturally gifted. She was big for her age and well-coordinated. She was a fast runner and could throw a ball farther than any of her teammates. Her skills were perfect for basketball and it soon became her favorite sport. She was so good that in sixth grade she was a star player on the girls' middle school team. She loved it when she was running down the court, dribbling the ball, and her family and the fans were yelling, "Go, Dana, go!"

Then, before she knew it, basketball season was over and it was time for softball. Softball was OK, but not as much fun as basketball. Then it was soccer season. "When does basketball start again?" she asked her coach.

"In a couple of weeks," he said. "Just keep practicing those free-throw shots at home. This should be a great season for you!"

Dana could hardly wait. "Mom! Dad! It's only a couple of weeks until basketball season," she announced at suppertime.

"Good," said her dad. "I guess we'll have to start canceling our Saturday night activities so we can watch your games."

"It's going to be a great season," Dana said proudly. "That's what the coach told me."

"Well, you've certainly been practicing. You should be ready—especially when it comes to shooting baskets."

After school a few days later, Dana was waiting for her mom, an elementary school teacher, to finish getting her classroom ready for the next day. It was sometimes tough having to wait. Most of the time, Dana worked on her homework, but today was a beautiful sunny day. "Mom, can I go out on the playground for a while?" Dana asked.

"Sure, Dana, just be careful because there's no one out there to supervise."

"No problem, Mom. I'll be careful."

She *was* careful at first, as she climbed around on the jungle gym and hung on the monkey bars. *I wonder how high I can pump*, she thought as she began swinging on the tall swings.

Pump, pump, pump, her legs and body went back and forth, forcing the swing higher and higher. *Whooo!* This was great! That's when Dana thought, *I bet I'm high enough that I could jump out of the swing, do a flip on the way down, and land on my feet*. She had seen a stunt like that on TV. She watched the

Photo taken by: Lichelle Olivera

athletes doing flips on all kinds of things—dirt bikes, skis, and skateboards. *How hard could it be?*

Without giving it a second thought, she let go of the chains, leaned forward, tucked her head, and began what she thought was a spectacular flip. The problem was the landing. Her feet didn't get as far around as they should in order to land correctly. Instead, she hit the ground with a huge thud, landing on her heels! Suddenly, a sharp pain went from her foot all the way to her brain. She screamed in agony.

At first, she was glad no one had seen her because she would have been embarrassed. On second thought, since no one had seen her or heard her scream, the only way to get help was for her to hop on her good foot all the way to her mom's classroom.

Mom examined Dana's foot. She didn't have medical training, but it didn't seem to be broken. By the time they got home, Dana's foot didn't hurt as much. But the minute Dana's heel touched the floor, pain shot through her body.

The next day was the same. The only way she could step on her foot was by walking on her toes. That's when Mom and Dad decided something was seriously wrong and took her to the doctor for an X-ray.

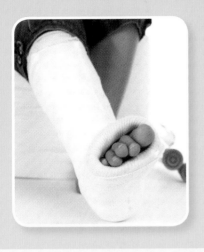

The doctor said that Dana had chipped her heel and he put a cast on her foot all the way to her knee. "Don't worry," he said, "you'll be fine in about six weeks."

"Six weeks? You mean, I'll miss the first six weeks of the basketball season?"

"I'm afraid so," sympathized the doctor.

"But trying to do a flip out of a swing is a pretty risky thing to do," Dad added. "Maybe this will help you think twice before you try being a daredevil again."

Dad was right. After that, whenever Dana was tempted to try something risky, she remembered hobbling around on crutches and missing six weeks of the basketball season. Dana quickly decided that her new motto should be "Better safe than sorry!" ∎

"If you know these things,
blessed are you if you do them."
—John 13:17, NKJV

MBBS4—9

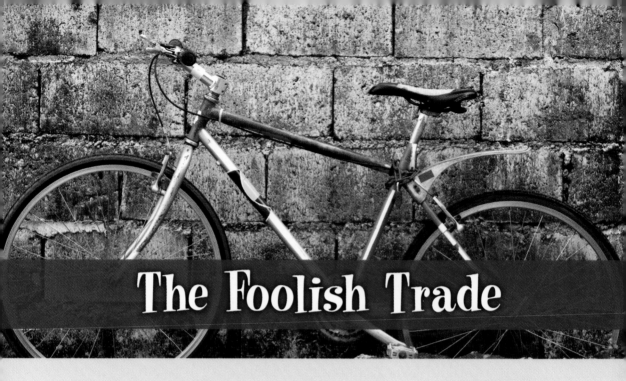

The Foolish Trade

When Jared was ten, his grandfather came to visit him from California. "I brought you something I thought you might like," smiled Grandpa.

Jared reached into a brown paper bag and pulled out what looked like a boxcar.

"Here, open this one." His Grandpa handed him another bag. Inside was an engine. Another bag held a caboose.

By the time Jared finished opening all of the bags, he had two train sets and plenty of track to hook them together. "Wow!" exclaimed Jared. "I must be the luckiest kid in the world!"

Grandpa explained that the two sets had belonged to Jared's uncles when they were kids, but since they didn't have boys of their own, they wanted Jared to have them.

"Will you please show me how this all goes together, Grandpa?" Jared pleaded eagerly.

In no time, Grandpa and Jared had the train *chug—chug—chugging* around a track, over a trestle, and past a miniature train station.

"Wow! This is so cool, Grandpa!" Jared exclaimed again and again.

Each day of Grandpa's visit the two would play with the train sets, occasionally changing a bit of the track or adding something like a house or a farm set with plastic animals to make it even more realistic.

After a few weeks, it was time for Grandpa to return home. "Take good care of your train set. It will last you for years. And who knows, someday you may be able to give it to your own son—or maybe a nephew."

Jared played with his train set everyday, but it wasn't quite as much fun playing alone. And the days were getting warmer, so Jared was spending a lot more time outdoors.

One day, his friend Paul came over and the two boys spent a couple of hours playing with Jared's trains. After that, Jared and Paul rode their bikes on the trails behind his house.

They hadn't gone far when Jared's bike began having problems. The axle just wasn't turning. Jared had to drag his bike back home with the tire skidding all the way.

"You're going to need a new axle," his father told him after he examined the problem. "When I get my next paycheck, I'll get you one and then I'll show you how to fix your own bike."

The very next day, Paul rode up on a brand-new bicycle. It was a ten-speed. "Hi Jared! Like my new bike?" he questioned.

The Foolish Trade

"Do I ever!" He examined it closer. "Mind if I take it for a spin?"

"Hop on!" insisted Paul.

Jared pulled a wheelie and then zoomed around the block before racing it back to his friend.

"Wow! This beauty handles the corners perfectly!" beamed Jared.

"Hey, want to go riding?" Paul suggested.

"Oh, my dad still hasn't gotten my bike fixed," Jared explained.

"No problem. You can ride my old bike," offered his friend.

Soon, with their mothers' permission, the two headed off on to the trails again. Jared had ridden Paul's old bike before and he had always noticed how much faster it went than his own. He could almost keep up with Paul's new ten-speed bike.

At the end of their ride, Paul made a surprising suggestion to Jared.

"Hey Jared, would you be willing to trade your train sets for my old bike?" his friend asked.

Jared didn't know what to think of such an offer. True, he had wanted a new bike for some time. Paul's wasn't new, but at least it was newer than his, and it went faster than his too. It was a hard decision. Finally, Jared thought he would rather have a bike to ride on than to just sit and watch a train go around and around on a track.

"OK, Paul, I'll trade with you," he agreed.

Jared helped carry armload after armload of train parts up to his friend's house. Then he rode his *new* used bike down to his place.

A short time after that, he was stretched out on the couch, watching TV when he heard his mother answer a phone call.

From his side of the conversation, Jared heard, "Hello, Clarissa." She listened for a few minutes to Paul's mom, then covered the receiver with her hand and called, "Jared, what's Paul's old bike doing out in our driveway?"

Just then, it occured to Jared that maybe before making the trade, he should have asked his mother.

"I traded Paul his old bike for the trains Grandpa gave me," he replied.

"You *what*?" his mom responded in disbelief.

"I traded the trains for Paul's old bike," Jared stated.

Mom turned back to the phone. "No, Clarissa, he doesn't need to bring them back. No, you're right. It wasn't a very fair deal, but Jared needs to learn a lesson from this."

For some reason Jared was starting to get the idea that the trade he had made wasn't exactly the smartest thing he had ever done in his life.

After she hung up, his mom said in a serious voice, "Jared, we need to talk." Jared went into the kitchen and sat down.

"Why did you trade your train sets for Paul's old bike?" asked his mother.

"Mom, my bike isn't working. And even when it gets fixed, it will never be as fast as Paul's old bike."

"Jared, you should *not* have traded something that your grandfather gave you as a gift." His mother continued, "Those train sets are collector's items. Someday they will be worth a great deal of money. Not only that, but both of those sets belonged to my brothers when they were growing up. It would have been nice to have kept them in the family."

Jared looked down at the floor. *If only I had asked Mom first,* he thought.

"Jared, Paul's mom realized you made a mistake, and she was willing to bring the train sets back, but I told her you needed to learn a lesson,"

Jared's mom stated. "Now, you need to call your Grandpa on the phone and tell him what you did."

Jared couldn't believe his ears. How could he tell Grandpa? But his mom was dialing the number, so he knew he would have some explaining to do.

"Hello, Grandpa?"

"Hello, Jared, are you enjoying the trains?"

"Grandpa, that's what I called to tell you about." He grasped for words. "I traded the trains for a bike."

"Did I hear you correctly? You traded the trains for a bike?"

"Yes, Grandpa, I'm so sorry," he responded meekly.

There was silence. Then his grandfather said sadly, "Well . . . they were your trains. I gave them to you. They were yours to do with as you wanted."

When Jared hung up the phone, he went quietly to his room. He wanted to be alone. Grandpa had forgiven him, but he wanted Jesus to forgive him too. Kneeling by his bed, he prayed, *Dear Jesus, how could I have been so foolish. Why didn't I think about how Grandpa would feel? I know he forgave me for trading his special trains, but I could hear in his voice that he was disappointed in me. Please forgive me. And help Grandpa not to be so sad . . . and help me to make better decisions. I love You, Jesus. Amen.*

For worship that night, Mom read the story in the Bible about a very foolish trade. It happened between two brothers. In fact, they were twins. Jacob had just finished cooking a large pot of lentils when his brother, Esau, came home from a hunting trip and was starved. Those beans smelled so delicious and he was so hungry that he could have devoured the whole pot right then and there. But Jacob said, "Hey, not so fast.

Those are my beans. What are you going to give me for them?" Esau, not wanting to wait another second to eat, said, "I'll give you whatever you want." And that's how Esau lost his birthright. He traded it for a pot of beans.

Jared thought about that story as he lay in bed that night. He envisioned the old, rusty bike lying in the driveway—the bike he had foolishly swapped for two very valuable train sets. *My own pot of beans,* he thought as he shook his head, *how foolish!*

The next morning, there was a knock at the door. Jared could hardly believe his eyes. There stood Paul and right behind him was a wagon . . . filled with Grandpa's trains!

"I didn't sleep very well last night," Paul said. "The trade we made yesterday wasn't fair. Your trains are worth a lot more than my bike and I've brought them back. I'm really sorry."

"I'm sorry too. I should have asked my mom first. I have your bike in the garage. I'll go get it." Jared started down the steps.

"No, that's OK. Keep the bike until you get yours fixed," Paul suggested.

"Really? That would be great! Are you sure?" Jared asked.

"Yup! I'm sure! I'd rather have a friend than a train set!"

"Or . . . a pot of beans!" Jared laughed.

"A what?" Paul looked confused.

"Let's go set up my trains, and I'll tell you all about it." Jared said, still laughing. "It's a great story about a foolish trade!" ∎

> *"Do not store up for yourselves treasures on earth, where moth and rust destroy."*
> —Matthew 6:19, NIV

Gate Mistake

"Let's see . . . do we have everything we need for our hike?" Dad checked each of the backpacks. "This is Mom's . . . with the lunch. Here's mine with the water bottles. This one with the binoculars is Tristan's. And here is Libby's with the Band-Aids—and the book she's been reading!" Dad chuckled. "That looks like everything we need. I'll just get the map and my compass and we'll be ready!"

Dad spread out his map of England's Lake District on a picnic table and showed Tristan and Libby where they were going. He explained that the pale blue shape on the map was a lake called Coniston Water, and the little yellow wiggly line was the trail to the top of the hill. "The hill has a funny name," he commented. "The Old Man of Coniston!" Libby laughed.

The trail was quite steep. Libby already felt tired just looking at the hill ahead. It seemed like a long way to the top. After hiking for almost an hour, they reached a gate across the trail that seemed to be locked. "Oh no," said Libby, "now we'll have to go all the way back down again!"

"Well," said Mom, "I'm sure we can open it. These farm gates all fasten differently. See if you can figure it out."

Tristan and Libby ran to the gate and tried to open it. Tristan noticed there was a chain that had to be lifted over the gatepost. The gate opened and they quickly ran through.

"Kids!" Dad called. "Come back. I need to show you something!"

Libby and Tristan ran back to the gate. "An important rule of the countryside is to make sure that whenever you open a gate, you must always close it again properly."

"Why's that, Dad?" asked Tristan.

"Because country gates are there to keep the animals safe by preventing them from wandering on to the roads or into fields full of plants they shouldn't eat."

Soon they came to another gate. It opened by pulling a stiff lever. Dad came to help them. After everyone had gone through, Tristan and Dad pushed the gate back and clicked the lever into the closed position.

Tristan turned to Dad and said, in a Dad kind of voice, "One of the most important rules in the countryside is to make sure that every time you open a gate, you must always close it again properly!" Dad laughed. He was glad Tristan was learning an important lesson in a fun way.

After a while, there was another gate, and then another. Libby and

Tristan took turns opening the gates before Mom and Dad arrived and closed them again afterwards. Tristan would always say to Libby, in his funny, low voice, "Don't forget to close the gate!" And Libby would always laugh at him.

They were getting near the top of the hill now. Tristan remembered his grated carrot and peanut butter sandwiches and the oatmeal cookies they had baked yesterday. "Mom, can we stop soon and have some lunch?"

"Yes, when we get to the top of the hill. I'm getting hungry too!"

Soon they reached the last gate. Dad opened it and everyone walked through. "Those flat rocks over there look like a good place to have lunch!" said Mom.

On the other side of the gate, Dad checked the map again. "I'm not sure which trail we should take from here. Should we go this way," he asked as he pointed at the map, "and back down through the woods? Or should we go this way and along the waterfall?"

Mom looked at the map too. "I think the waterfall sounds nice."

Tristan's stomach rumbled. He turned to Libby. "Race you to the rock!" Mom took off her backpack and untied the top. "Here are your sandwiches, kids. *Mmm,* I'm really hungry! Libby, will you say grace, please?"

As soon as Libby finished praying, Mom opened her eyes and yelled, "Oh, no! We forgot to shut the gate!"

Tristan was about to run back and close the gate when he realized it was too late. More sheep than he had ever seen before were racing, as fast as sheep can run, toward the open gate! The rest of the flock followed until the trail on the other side of the gate was full of sheep! They were running and jumping down the hill like a woolly river!

Dad had already started running towards the gate, but the sheep ran faster. If only he could get in front of them so he could chase them back up the hill. But the sheep completely filled the trail, making it impossible.

Dad didn't know what to do. He ran through the field alongside the trail, hoping they had remembered to shut the next gate properly. When he reached the second gate, the sheep were already there and he had to climb over a thornbush to get in front of them. The sheep were big and some had large horns. He was worried that they might hurt him as they raced forward.

Mom and the children watched helplessly. Mom prayed out loud, "Please God, don't let Dad get hurt! And please help us to know what to do about the sheep."

She sat down on the rock and put her arms around Libby and Tristan. Dad was trying to shoo the sheep back up the hill, but they didn't seem to understand anything he said or did! Or, if they did understand, they were in no mood to obey! Libby began to cry and Tristan continued to pray. They had tried so hard to close every gate properly, but they had all been too busy thinking about eating lunch when they came through the very last one.

Suddenly, they saw the shepherd running after the sheep. Tristan was worried that the man would be angry with them for not shutting the gate. The shepherd whistled. Quick as a flash, one of his dogs ran through the field and jumped into the trail next to Dad. Almost immediately, the sheep nearest the dog turned around, and soon the sheep began to run back up the trail, through the open gate, and into their own field.

Dad came running up the hill behind the sheep and met the shepherd at the top gate. "I'm so sorry," he said breathlessly. "I feel very foolish because all the way up the trail I was teaching my children how important it is to make sure to always shut the gates. And then, when we got to the top—we all forgot!"

The shepherd smiled kindly. "Don't worry!" he said. "It happens all the time! That's why we have so many gates on the trail! The dogs know exactly what to do and the sheep obey them. So, just enjoy your lovely day!" The shepherd smiled again, waved at the children, and walked toward his sheep.

"He was a very nice shepherd," said Tristan. "He was kind and patient with us—and look how kind and patient he was when all those sheep were trying to escape."

"And he's very forgiving too!" said Dad. "I expected a lecture, but I think he knew that we had already learned a valuable lesson about being more careful."

"Yes," said Mom, "those sheep are fortunate. He is a very good shepherd."

"Just like Jesus!" said Libby.

"Yes," Mom agreed, "Jesus is the best Shepherd of all." ■

> *The LORD is my shepherd; I shall not want.*
> —Psalm 23:1, NKJV

Hannah's Dream Doll

Photo taken by: Laura Richardson

H annah had seen the doll on television. The minute she saw her, she couldn't think of anything else. She even dreamed about her. Hannah had already named the doll Rebecca Lynn because she thought that was the prettiest name in the whole world—and certainly fitting for the prettiest doll in the whole world.

The problem was, Hannah didn't have enough money to buy the doll, and she knew her parents were struggling just to pay the mortgage so the family would have a home to live in. An expensive doll at this time was a luxury that cost way too much.

After a few days of thinking about Rebecca Lynn, Hannah got up the courage to tell her mother about the doll. "Mom, I saw the most beautiful doll on television the other day, and I'd really like to buy her. She has long red hair and a beautiful porcelain face. Please, can I have her?"

"How much is she?" Mom asked.

"Well, I don't know how much she

costs, but I was thinking that maybe I could get her for my birthday . . . or for Christmas."

"Hannah, I'm glad you've found a doll that you really like. And it's OK to dream. But you know that Dad and I don't have much money right now, so we really have to watch what we buy."

"But Mom, they said on TV that it's on sale for half price right now. And you can make three easy payments. Please, can we buy her?" Hannah pleaded.

"Well, right now, that's not possible, but maybe, if you plan carefully, you can save enough money to buy the doll. I'll try to think of some special jobs that you can do around the house to earn a little extra."

That night, when Hannah went to bed, she thought to herself, *At least Mom didn't say No!* She knelt down by her bed, "Dear Jesus," she prayed, "You know how much I want Rebecca Lynn. And Dad's always telling me about the text in the Bible that says God can do anything. So, please, dear Jesus, help me to find the money I need. Thank You. Amen."

The very next day, Hannah was invited to go to the park with her best friend, Rochelle. The girls had a wonderful time playing on the playground and feeding bread to the ducks. When one of the ducks grabbed a whole slice of bread, Hannah ran after the duck to try to catch it. Suddenly,

she saw something strange partially buried in the dry leaves. *What is that?* she asked herself. She reached down and picked up a little black purse. *I wonder what's inside?*

When Hannah opened the purse, she couldn't believe her eyes. It was filled with money. It looked like enough to buy Rebecca Lynn. *Was this an answer to her prayer?* she wondered.

Quickly, she shut the purse and ran back to Rochelle. "Rochelle!

Rochelle, I think God just answered my prayer! Remember the doll I've been wanting? Well, last night I prayed that Jesus would help me get the money to buy her, and look what I found!"

"Wow, that's a lot of money!" Rochelle gasped as she peeked into the purse. "Don't you think you should try to find the person who lost it?"

"Kinda," Hannah admitted, "but this could be an answer to my prayer. Maybe it's meant for me!"

"Or maybe it isn't!" Rochelle said thoughtfully.

When Hannah got home, she didn't tell her parents about the purse. Emptying the contents out on her bed, she counted the money. Fifty dollars! *Why, that's enough for Rebecca Lynn,* she thought. Then she searched inside the purse to see if she could find who it belonged to. There was no name anywhere. *What should I do?* she questioned. She was confused. She knelt by her bed and prayed again. "Dear Jesus, thank You for letting me find this money. Please help me decide if I should keep it or try to find the owner. Amen."

Photo taken by: Laura Richardson

She tossed and turned that night, struggling with what she should do. Finally, her decision was made. At breakfast, Hannah told her parents all about her prayer that Jesus would help her find the money to buy Rebecca Lynn, and then she told them about the purse she had found. "Look at all the money that's inside," she said as she held it out for them to see. "I really, really want to keep it, but I think Jesus wants me to try to find the owner. What should I do?" she asked.

"Let's go by the police station and ask if anyone has reported a lost purse," Dad suggested. When they arrived at the station, they told the policeman at the desk about the purse. He shuffled through some papers and said, "Two days ago we received a report that a little girl lost her purse that was filled with birthday money from her grandparents. She will be very happy to get this back." Hannah slowly handed the purse to the policeman. She was glad she had given the money back, but was sad now that she wouldn't be able to get Rebecca Lynn.

A few days later, when Mom answered the phone, she called, "Hannah, it's for you. It's the girl who lost the purse."

"Hi. My name's Abby. Thank you for giving back my money," she said. "I thought I would never see it again."

"I'm glad I returned it," Hannah replied. "When I found your purse, I prayed that Jesus would tell me what I should do. I really wanted to buy a new doll with the money, but after praying, I knew that I should try to find who the purse belonged to."

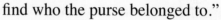

Photo taken by Laura Richardson

"Oh, I've been wanting a new doll too! What kind do you want?"

And then Hannah told Abby all about Rebecca Lynn.

Three days later, a mail carrier rang the bell. Hannah ran to the door. She was surprised when the man handed her a big package. "Mom, it's for me!" Hannah exclaimed. "Can I open it now?"

"Of course," said Mom.

Inside was a note that read, "Dear Hannah, Thank you for being so honest. I hope you enjoy this present. Love, Abby's grandmother."

Hannah tore through the wrappings and there was Rebecca Lynn, her very own dream doll. God had answered her prayer. ■

Do not withhold good from those who deserve it, when it is in your power to act.
—Proverbs 3:27, NIV

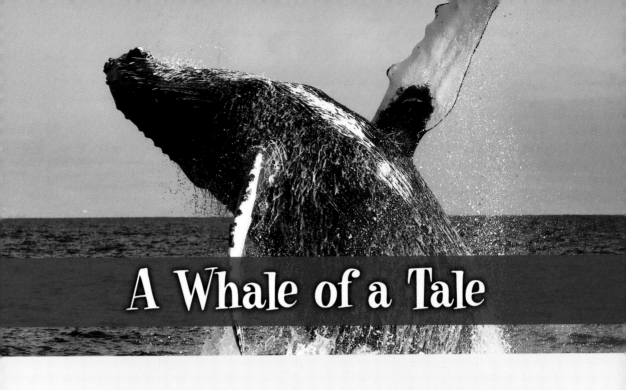

A Whale of a Tale

"Greg! Sheila!" Mom called from her writing desk in the family room when she noticed the kids trying to sneak out the front door. "It's time to write those thank-you notes. It's already the middle of January and the relatives are going to be wondering if you received the gifts they sent. And they'll want to know how you liked them. It's important to say thank you. It's the polite thing to do."

"But Mom, we're heading over to Ben's house. He has something he wants to show us. We'll do it later."

"Just a minute, kids. You've been saying, 'Later,' every time I've reminded you. I want you to get those notes written today. When someone does something nice for you, you should get into the habit of saying *thank you* immediately—not three months later!"

"It hasn't been three months," Greg said, "and we already told most of the people thank you over the phone. Isn't that enough?"

"Well, it's nice that you remembered to call them, but it's really, really special when you take the time to actually write a thank-you note and send it."

"OK, when we get back I'll e-mail a note. It will be easy—just copy and paste. And I have almost everyone's e-mail address," Greg said.

"That's not good enough," Mom held firm to her first request. "You need to actually write a handwritten note of thanks to each person who gave you a gift. I have note cards you can use. Or better yet, why don't you design each card yourselves. That would even make it more personal."

"But Mom," Sheila complained. "That's old-fashioned. I bet you're the only parent in the state of Nebraska who still makes their kids write handwritten notes."

"Maybe so," Mom said. "But just think . . . if that's true, then you will be the most polite kids in Nebraska!"

"Awww, Mom."

"Don't 'awww Mom' me! Just call Ben and tell him you'll be over later. Tell him your mom is in the middle of teaching you a lesson in good manners!"

Sheila called Ben. He was busy doing chores, so he said later was just fine. Mom got out some blank paper along with some colored markers and spread them out on the kitchen table. She told the kids to first make a list of everyone who gave them a gift and then write down what the gift was, so they could check off each name when that note was finished.

When Greg and Sheila sat down and started making their lists, Mom could tell they weren't very happy about it. What could she do to change their *attitude* to one of *cheerful gratitude*? Suddenly, it came to her.

"Kids, what you need is a whale of a tale," she announced.

"A *what?*"

"Yes," said Mom, "let me see if I can find that picture of a whale that I found when I was surfing the Web. Ahhh, yes," she announced a few minutes later. "Here it is."

The kids eagerly left their writing project and looked over their mom's shoulder at a picture of a fifty-foot whale upright in the water. A diver, next to the whale, looked like a teeny, tiny man. "Now let me tell you the story of this whale," Mom said.

"A few years ago, a fisherman close to San Francisco saw a large, probably fifty-ton, female humpback whale that had gotten tangled in some crab pot lines. He realized that without help she would die, so he called a marine rescue station that sent out some divers to see what they

could do. 'We'll have to get into the water and cut those lines,' the first diver announced . . . and jumped in. The others followed, knowing that with one whack of her powerful tail, they could be killed.

"That's when they realized that the whale had gotten twisted up in about twenty heavy crab pot lines, each two hundred and forty feet long with weights every sixty feet. In addition, there were about twelve crab pots, weighing close to one hundred pounds each hanging from the whale. The ropes were wrapped around her tail four times and were cutting into her blubber. Without immediate help, she wouldn't be able to keep her blowhole above the water to breathe.

"It took more than an hour working with large curved knives to cut the ropes that held the whale. And the amazing thing is that, all the time the men were around her cutting away the ropes, she didn't make a move— she just watched them with her great big eyes. But what's even more amazing is what the whale did when the last line was cut and she was free. Instead, of getting out of there as quickly as possible, she joyfully swam circles around the divers. Then she came back to each diver, one at a time, and nudged him gently as if thanking him.

"So kids, if a whale can cheerfully say *thank you* in a personal way, so can you."

"Wow, that's some story," Sheila said, shaking her head in amazement. "I guess if a whale knows how to say thank you, I can too."

"It's like God created animals to not only be cheerful givers—but cheerful receivers. Hey, let's get on with writing those thank-you notes. We can be cheerful receivers too," Greg announced.

"Thanks, Mom," Sheila said. "That was a great whale of a tale!" ■

> *And whatever you do in word or deed, do all in the name of the Lord Jesus, giving thanks to God the Father through Him.*
> —Colossians 3:17, NKJV

Pam's Praying Mantis

"No pets!" Pam's mother was adamant. "No animals in this house and that's that!"

"But, Mom," Pam pleaded, "all of my friends have pets. Just one? Please, Mom. I'll take care of it all by myself. I promise."

"Sorry, Pam. I mean it." Mom put her hand on Pam's shoulder.

"I know how much you love animals, but, not in this house. They are just too much work! I'm very sorry."

Pam had always loved animals. From the time she was very young, she had been naturally drawn to them. She read about them, studied about them, and had stuffed animals of all kinds in her room. Now she wanted her very own pet. She didn't care what it was. Why, she would even settle for . . .

And at that moment, Pam had the best idea ever. She had just finished reading an article about a man in Texas who kept a praying mantis for a pet.

Pam wondered how her mother

would respond if she asked to keep a praying mantis as a pet. She had an old aquarium in her room. It was time to find out.

"Mom," Pam began, "I have an idea."

"What's that?" Mom stopped dusting and turned toward her daughter.

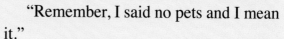

"Remember, I said no pets and I mean it."

"I know, Mom. But, maybe this will work as a compromise." Pam's eyes lit up with hope.

"Go ahead. I'm listening." Her mother looked at her warily.

Photo: canstockphoto.com

"I was reading about this man in Texas. He kept an unusual pet. I was thinking . . ."

"No snakes, either." Pam's mother shuddered.

"No, not a snake . . . a praying mantis." Pam finished quickly.

"A *what*?"

"A praying mantis. You know, it's a bug, usually about three or four inches long, and I can find one outside so it wouldn't cost anything."

"A bug? You want to bring a bug into this house?" Mom looked at her daughter as if she had just suggested the wildest thing she could imagine. "You know I hate bugs." Her mother had made that clear—with a can of bug spray in every room!

"I know, Mom, but this bug would be different. I'd keep the praying mantis in an aquarium with a screen on top so it couldn't get out. They're gentle. They don't bite or get into things. They're really, really neat."

"Show me a picture of one." Mom followed her daughter to the computer where Pam typed in the words "praying mantis."

"See," Pam said as she pointed to the screen. "Aren't they amazing?" Pam was full of enthusiasm. "God made them special. They are the only bug that can turn their heads from side to side, almost one hundred and eighty degrees. They have amazing eyesight and can see up to fifty feet away. And, Mom, their name in Greek means *prophet*. They even look like they're praying. That's how they get their name. Oh please, Mom.

It won't hurt anything. And since they eat bugs, they're easy to feed. I'll take good care of it. Please?"

Mom looked from the picture to her daughter. She had to admit that it looked like a very interesting bug.

"Well, if you keep it in its cage I guess I'll let you try it, just this once. I don't want it jumping around the house!"

Pam gave her mom a great big hug. "Thanks so much! You won't be sorry, I promise!"

Pam spent the next week carefully combing through the grass. It was a tough job since praying mantises are masters of disguise. They can adapt their colors to the plants they are on, so they are difficult to find. Pam looked around the flower garden where other insects thrived since that is what the mantises eat. Finally, late on Friday afternoon, Pam spotted an adult mantis chewing happily on its supper.

"Hey, I'll call you Daniel— because the Bible says that Daniel prayed three times a day and you always look like you're praying." She scooted the three-inch bug slowly into her hand. His antennae moved wildly around his head, trying to smell this new creature that had invaded his world.

Pam had the aquarium ready for Daniel. She had added some grass and an area of water, and had even placed a small moth and a cricket in the aquarium so Daniel would have something to hunt and eat. He was an unusual pet, but, at least, Daniel was hers. Her very first pet!

All summer long, as soon as Pam finished her chores, she would play with Daniel. First, she carried him on her hand to the front porch. Then she would sit and talk to him and watch as he would rotate his head back and forth as if he understood what she was saying. She loved feeding

him bits of tuna that she stuck on a toothpick. He would remove each bit from the tip and hold it in his long legs. After eating, Pam let him drink water from an old teaspoon.

But what she enjoyed most was watching Daniel pray. In church she remembered a sermon about how you should pray all the time. She had written down the text: " 'Pray without ceasing,' 1 Thessalonians 5:17." She had tried it for a while, but then she would forget. Daniel, however, changed all that. Now, whenever she looked at Daniel, she remembered to pray. Sometimes she prayed for her friends. Sometimes she prayed that Jesus would help her do her best at school. And sometimes she prayed for poor people around the world who didn't have any food to eat. But mostly she prayed for opportunities to witness for Jesus.

It was late in the fall, and Pam had hurried home from school. She put her homework on the table and went to check on Daniel. Usually, when she came into the room, he would turn his great head toward her, anticipating her approach. Today, he wasn't moving. Pam knew that this day would come. She knew that praying mantises usually only lived about a year and Daniel had been an adult when she found him. Tears came to her eyes. She had grown to love her praying mantis and was sad that he had died.

Even Mom had grown fond of the big green bug. And she felt sorry for her daughter. Suddenly, she knew what she was going to do to make Pam smile again. She had seen on the Internet that it was possible to purchase mantis egg cases. She happily ordered three, hoping that at least one would hatch for her precious daughter. That way, Pam could raise a praying mantis from the time it was a baby nymph.

Finally, the day came when the package with the three egg cases was

delivered. Mom was so excited that she was waiting at the door smiling when the school bus dropped Pam off.

"I have a surprise for you, honey!" Mom exclaimed.

"Really? What is it?" Pam looked suprised.

"Open it and see," her mother urged as she handed the box to Pam. "I felt bad after you lost Daniel, so, I ordered you another praying mantis. Actually, I ordered three egg cases, just to make sure at least one survived."

"Mom. You didn't! Three cases? But, that could mean . . ." Pam had already slit open the box and was lifting one of the flaps. Somehow, something had gone wrong. The box that should have remained cold until spring had gotten warm during shipping, and the cases had broken open. Suddenly, hundreds of little green nymphs began to swarm from the box, each one a miniature version of Daniel. They landed on the walls, the table, and even in the glass of lemonade Mom had given to Pam. Soon they were spreading throughout the house.

Pam and her mother began to laugh. Mom had assumed that each egg case carried one tiny nymph, but instead there were more than four hundred in each case.

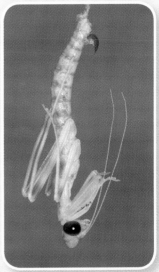

Pam and her mother ran through the house with a butterfly net and a box, trying to catch the little creatures that were jumping everywhere. "Quick! Shut the door to my bedroom," Mom yelled. "I don't want to sleep with bugs tonight!"

As fast as Pam's net was full, she would run outside and shake the little nymphs into the yard. Then back in she would go for another load.

"You know, Mom," Pam smiled as she placed the last of the tiny mantises in the grass in their front yard, "I have been praying that Jesus would give me opportunities to witness for Him. Maybe all these praying mantises will remind people to pray, just like Daniel did for me."

Mom looked at her daughter and smiled. "I think Jesus did answer your prayer. God doesn't always answer in the way you think He will. But He does hear you when you pray—and He does answer!" ■

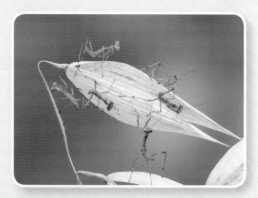

Pray without ceasing.
—1 Thessalonians 5:17, NKJV

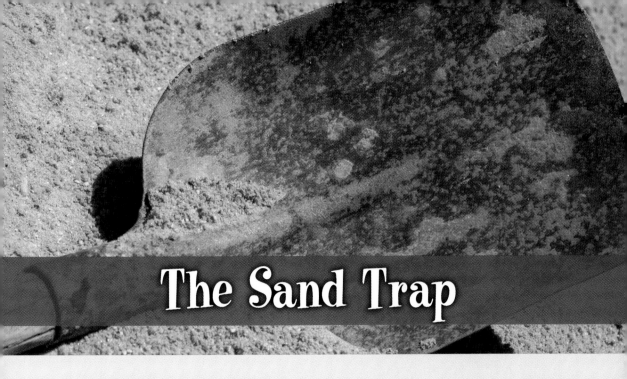

The Sand Trap

"Hurry up, Jackson! Mr. Bailey is waiting for us." Tyrone was already heading out to the old station wagon that his parents allowed him to drive. This was the first summer with his license, and he loved the freedom it had given him. He was even able to take odd jobs, like helping Mr. Bailey.

"I'm coming!" Jackson sluggishly followed behind. "It's blistering hot out here, and it's still early. Why do you have to always choose the hottest days to help that man? And why did you have to volunteer my services? If you would have asked me first, I could have told you that this week was going to be a scorcher."

"Oh, come on, Jackson, you know lots of things, but let's face it, you're not always right," Tyrone teased.

"Well, I'm right at least ninety-nine percent of the time!" Jackson laughed.

"Let's get going, I don't want to be late," Tyrone urged.

"We'd have plenty of time if you'd

The Sand Trap

just take the shortcut. It would probably shave ten minutes off our drive time."

Tyrone climbed into the driver's seat. "How many times have I heard that?" he said as he watched his brother get in beside him and buckle his seat belt. "It's not the shortcut that's the problem. It's the sand you've got to go through at the end before you reach the paved road." Tyrone backed out of the driveway and turned the car in the opposite direction.

"Are you sure you don't want to take the shortcut?" Jackson asked hopefully, knowing full well what the answer would be. Ever since the family had moved to their new home, Jackson had tried to talk them into trying the sandy road that could cut off several miles of their route around the neighborhood. His friend, Matt, lived on that road and they used it all

the time. Of course, they drove a great big truck with four-wheel drive, but Jackson didn't think that was a problem at all! He felt sure their small station wagon could handle it just fine! Matt teased him about it all the time and, just once, Jackson wanted to show his friend that they could do it. But Tyrone was not convinced. He just frowned and continued driving on the main road.

Mr. Bailey greeted the boys with a hardy handshake. "Thanks for coming. It shouldn't take long to move this dirt out to where I need it in the garden. I sure appreciate your help."

Tyrone grabbed a shovel and started filling the wheelbarrow. Jackson

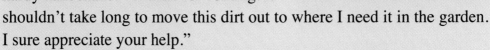

shoveled, too, just not as enthusiastically. Back and forth they went with the rich black dirt. They worked steadily and finished in record time.

"I want to thank you fellows for working so hard on such a hot day. You're worth what I promised you—and more. I put a little bonus in here for you," Mr. Bailey said with a twinkle in his eye as he handed each of them a check.

"Thanks, Mr. Bailey. We appreciate the work," Tyrone replied.

As they walked toward the old station wagon, Jackson looked at his watch. "Hey, Tyrone, we finished quicker than I thought. Would you mind taking me by Matt's place on the way home? I promised him I'd beat him in a game of one-on-one basketball if we got the job done in time!"

As they headed out of the driveway, Jackson realized they could get there even faster . . . if they took the shortcut.

"Tyrone," Jackson began, "we could cut off a lot of time if you took the shortcut." He tried to win Tyrone with his smile. They were at the Stop sign and it was time for a choice. Turn right and go the long way, or go straight and . . .

"I don't think our car can make it over that patch of sand," Tyrone replied. But he said it as if he wouldn't mind doing something daring just this once.

"It wouldn't hurt to take a look. Just *one* look? Come on, it's such a beautiful day. Let's live a little."

Tyrone struggled with his decision and, at the last second, steered the car straight across the road instead of taking a turn.

"Yeah, Tyrone!" Jackson smiled as they passed the No Outlet sign and then stopped to eye the sandy area that led to the shortcut and home. It was the only part that wasn't hard packed.

Jackson was too proud to give up without a fight.

"The shortcut is only fifteen feet past the sand. Our car can do that. Come on, Tyrone. I dare you!" Jackson knew his brother could hardly pass up a good-natured dare.

Tyrone briefly considered what he should do, then, without another word, he put the car in gear, revved the engine, and floored it. The little wagon tore through the sand for about six feet . . . then abruptly stopped!

Jackson looked at his brother who gave him one of his famous *I-told-you-so* looks.

"I'll go see what happened," Jackson said, feeling a little guilty, as he jumped out of the car.

"Good idea," he heard his brother mutter behind him.

Jackson looked to see which tire had buried itself in the sand. All

four tires looked the same—and they didn't seem to be buried that deep. "Put it in reverse. I'll push us right out." Jackson felt quite sure he had the answer. He pushed nonchalantly at first and then gave it all he had. The car didn't budge even an inch!

Tyrone lifted one eyebrow and looked at him as he started rolling up the windows and locking the doors. "Come on, let's go."

Tyrone gave Jackson another look and started walking down the sandy road.

"But, Tyrone. It's almost two miles on foot—and it must be almost ninety degrees out."

"Uh-huh."

Jackson felt miserable. It was bad enough to be stuck, but now they would have to walk right past Matt's house. *If he sees me I'll never hear the end of it!*

Then he had an idea. "I know a shorter way." Jackson pushed past Tyrone and headed into the thick of the woods. He turned around and watched to make sure Tyrone was following him. The sandy road would have been much easier, but way too embarrassing if Matt found out that Jackson was wrong. He wanted to avoid that at all costs!

They arrived home at the same time as their father, who had just finished a ten-hour shift. Jackson explained the problem. His father didn't question why the boys had been so foolish, he just sighed and shook his head slowly. After putting their shovels and boards into Dad's trunk, they climbed into the car and drove the long way around towards the sand trap.

It wasn't going to be easy. The chassis was buried and a lot of sand would have to be removed to get the boards in place. Jackson kept looking back over his shoulder, hoping that no one that knew him would come along and offer to help.

Dad and the boys shoveled and shoveled in the scorching heat. They finally managed to get boards under the wheels and were ready to try moving the car when they saw a red truck heading their way. *Oh no!* Jackson knew that truck. It was Matt and his father. The truck pulled to a stop next to the buried car.

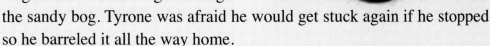

"Need some extra man-power?" Matt's dad asked as they got behind the wagon and pushed while Tyrone steered. The little wagon shot forward right through the sandy bog. Tyrone was afraid he would get stuck again if he stopped so he barreled it all the way home.

"Jackson, I'm sorry that you couldn't come over this afternoon," Matt said as he got into the truck next to his dad. Then they drove right through the sandy area with no problem at all. Dad wearily climbed into their car as Jackson got in beside him and buckled up. His father didn't say a word as they turned around and headed home. But Jackson knew exactly what he was thinking!

Finally, Jackson couldn't stand the silence any longer. "Dad, I'm really sorry. It's all my fault. I dared Tyrone to do it! I was just so sure we could make it!"

"Remember, son, that no one knows everything . . . except God! It never pays to be a know-it-all. God wants us to be humble. He also wants us to pray about everything! You won't ever be really happy until you let God lead and guide you through the *sand traps* in your life!"

"Thanks, Dad. And thanks for being so cool about it!"

Dad reached over and gently squeezed Jackson's shoulder, "I love you, son!" ∎

Do you see a man wise in his own eyes?
There is more hope for a fool than for him.
—Proverbs 26:12, NKJV